Unsettled

A MEMOIR

LAURIE WOODFORD

Unsettled: A Memoir

Published by Unsolicited Press.

Printed in the United States of America.

First Edition.

Attention schools and businesses: for discounted copies on large orders, please contact the publisher directly.

For information contact:

Unsolicited Press

Portland, Oregon

www.unsolicitedpress.com

orders@unsolicitedpress.com

619-354-8005

Front Cover Design: Kathryn Gerhardt

Editor: Summer Stewart

ISBN: 978-1-956692-85-3

For my dad, with love and admiration

In the interest of privacy, some names of individuals, places, streets and institutions have been changed. This is a true story told from my rather quirky perspective. Some people who appear as characters in this book might recall events, interactions, and conversations quite differently. That's the nature of memory. Along the way, I may have gotten a fact or two wrong or offered up a misguided interpretation of a situation. That's human nature. But I did my best. My hope is that any reader who recognizes him or herself on the page finishes the book with a smile.

Table of Contents

Unsettled

A MEMOIR

Part I

Mount Hope

I was a forty-eight-year-old divorcee living in Rochester, New York, when I went on a Match.com coffee date, one afternoon, with a man who had a wandering eye. He'd telephoned a few days before we met. "This is Jim from Match," he'd said. "Let's say Saturday. Two o'clock. Starbucks." Jim was rather directive. "The Starbucks near Elmwood and Winton," he'd added. "Not Elmwood and Mount Hope." Apparently, a former date had gotten the two locations confused.

In the entranceway of Starbucks, I scanned tables searching for a man resembling the photographed images Jim had posted on his online dating profile. I didn't have much to go on. In his close-up photo, Jim's face appeared non-descript. Clean-shaven. Light eyes. Brown hair. In another photo, Jim stood in a doorway wearing loose jeans and white baseball cap. I'd studied that photograph, thinking somehow it might offer insight into the man I was about to meet. He looked pleasant, almost fun-loving. His profile stated he was six-foot, one. I studied the photo again. Maybe it was a trick door, and, in reality, he was five-foot, three.

From a corner table, Jim lifted his chin and waved. Then stood. About six-foot, one. *Normal door.* "You must be Laurie," he said.

"Nice to meet you, Jim." I smiled then sat in the chair across from him. That was when I noticed his wandering eye. It wasn't that he looked at other women. He had an ophthalmologically diagnosed wandering eye. Strabismus or tropia, they call it. I found this in no way unattractive. But I needed a moment or two to orient myself, figure out the best approach to making eye contact. Then I quickly settled my gaze on his stationary eye as we chatted about weather and hobbies and road construction on Mount Hope.

Then Jim started talking at length about his work as an electrician. PVC bodies. Elbows. Closed nipples. Rigid conduits. Was he coming on to me? All the while, his one peeper focused on my face, and my breasts, while his other eye roamed. A freewheeler. Circling the Starbuck's menu board and bags of French roast near checkout.

Jim was relieved to see me in person. "Finally, a woman who actually looks like her photos." I'd posted a smiling head shot I'd cropped from a family Christmas photo. Also, a snapshot of me in muddied shorts feeding bamboo to an elephant in Thailand. In both, I had good hair. "I've had it up to here," Jim said, raising his palm above his head, "meeting women who look nothing like their pictures."

Jim had been on a series of one-time coffee dates with women who'd failed to thrill him. He'd met a woman who appeared svelte in her photographs. "But in person," Jim said, his voice swooping high and tight, "a good twenty pounds overweight." I glanced at my cell phone -- 2:19 p.m. Another woman was a solid brunette in her snapshots. In real life, "salt and pepper!" I tracked Jim's wandering eye -- hazel and orbed.

Watched it traverse the café. *Can it read the latte specials? Is it checking out the cashier's lip piercing?* "Another woman was very nice-looking in her photos." Jim sipped his Columbian brew. "When I walked into the restaurant, I hardly recognized her! She was just frumpy…"

Online dating let down. Jim had taken the time to put on a clean shirt and trim his nose hair. And for what?

I'd experienced my share of first-meet disappointments. The man who'd written, "Family is everything to me!" still lived with his mother. The gentleman who'd boasted, "Women tell me I'm a great friend" confessed impotence. Before each coffee date, I'd carefully assessed my attire, refreshed my lip gloss, swiped on mascara. Then moments before meeting, I'd breathed a brief inhale of hopefulness, like a taste of mild, March air. Maybe. Maybe. The guy waiting for me beside the Starbucks's pastry case will be a match. A man with whom I'll share authentic connection. The man I'll talk with, sleep with, confide in, support. Doesn't hope feel good?

While Jim recited his agitations towards past dates, I thought back to his online photographs. The one of him in the doorway, standing and smiling, looking like a nice guy. The closeup of his face, in which his brown hair waved a bit above one ear and both eyes were looking straight ahead at the camera at the same time.

That was a year or so before my travels. Around the time my settled life in Rochester began feeling all too familiar, like the soft sweatpants I'd fish from my dresser drawer each Saturday morning and wear to the local grocers despite their pilled fabric, the hole in one knee. It was around the time an urgent restlessness began to pester me. First, during afternoon lulls in my daily work routine, then each evening as I sat on my sofa answering emails in front of the television. *Something's missing.*

At night, I'd awaken from deep sleep an hour before dawn. Sit with hot tea. Ask myself what I wanted, what I was longing for. My answer, at first, felt vague. Wholeness, perhaps? As months passed, my uneasiness took on momentum, snowballed into a compelling force. I felt a compulsion to seek, a drive to cast about, an explorer's itch. And I began toying with the idea of leaving my job, my house, my friends and family, the place that felt like home.

That was before I moved to South Korea to teach English at a university in Seoul and, later, in Daehag. Before I backpacked in Ethiopia and Peru and Fuerteventura. Then worked without a visa in Mexico for a while.

Four years in motion. Some might call it my mid-life crisis. Others my adventure. I say one thing led to another. Then another. While I explored the world. Grappled with the notion of home. Searched for love. Always looking. With one eye focused straight ahead. The other eye circling, circling, perusing the possibilities.

Lost Ovaries

South Korea felt anything but familiar with its Seoul street vendors who sold stewed silkworm larvae, mung bean pancakes, steamed octopus, and conch. Store signs were written in Hangul -- the Korean alphabet – in stacked letters that looked, to me, like tiny boxes and ladders, square-shaped S's and upside-down T's. Tanks of live flounder, eel and horseshoe crab lined sidewalks in front of restaurants and grocery stores. Green and yellow love birds sang from bamboo cages hung in tea house windows. The air in congested subway cars smelled of garlic, red chili paste, fermented cabbage. I navigated the crowded sidewalks and metro lines, the city river paths and jogging trails. Oftentimes, I felt disoriented and out of place, yet my skin tingled with a safari-hat sense of adventure.

Three months after arriving in South Korea, I decided my vagina needed to be looked at by a professional, for a change, and I made an appointment to part my knees for Dr. Cheong. I'd never been pap smeared in the Eastern Hemisphere yet approached the clinic reception desk with a swagger of confidence. How different could it be?

Dr. Cheong's clinic sat on the top floor of a squat three-story building bookended by high rises. A chipped incisor in a row of healthy teeth. The receptionist, a porcelain-skinned young woman with perfect facial symmetry, asked what I wanted "done." I hesitated, first because the question threw me, but also because the receptionist looked so familiar. *Hadn't I seen her somewhere before?* Then realized I'd seen that same face on my male English Composition student, Bumsuk.

In South Korea plastic surgery seemed stigma-free and commonplace. About half my students at Wangja University received cosmetic surgery promissory notes for high school graduation gifts. *Congratulations, Graduate! Anything is Possible!* Eyelid doubling, face fat thinning, jawbone reduction.

During an English conversation activity one day, my classroom full of bright, hardworking college freshmen confessed past or planned plastic surgeries. "What could you possibly want to change?" I'd asked, dumbfounded. Both male and female students rattled off perceived shortcomings. Too-round faces, slightly bumped noses, slit eyes.

There was an authentic sweetness about many of my students, an endearing naivety. "Have a nice weekend, Laurie teacher!" they'd say on Friday afternoons, holding their hands in front of their chests, fingers curved and thumbs touching. Hand hearts. "Thank you. Wonderful weekend to you, too." I'd smile and add, "Don't drink too much."

My heart would softly break over their misunderstanding -- that they needed to be something better when they were perfect as is. How could they not realize that the faces with which they were born, the way their features matured, blossomed – crinkled or dimpled, puckered or plumped – were uniquely expressive, golden, ideal?

Then I'd catch my own reflection in the sunlit classroom windowpane. My nose that looked roughly sculpted from Play Dough. The skin on my neck appearing tired and creased. My Willie Nelson ears. Why am *I* feeling sorry the *them*? They're so damned pretty! These Korean beauties with perfectly pouty lips on heart shaped faces. Their delicate trimmed-straight noses and pulled-round Kewpie eyes. Their Barbie doll chins and tiny moon shell ears. And those were the guys.

Dr. Cheong's receptionist wore a powder-pink jumper and nameplate with *Ji hee* in raised letters. Ji hee blinked at me. "You want gynecology or cosmetic?" Apparently, Dr. Cheong specialized in OBGYN and cosmetic surgery; she worked both ends. It was a business plan with foresight. Deliver a steady stream of "homely" babies. Eighteen years later, chisel them adorable.

"Uh, gynecology," I said. Ji hee placed a sheet of paper on the desk counter. Using the fingertips of both hands, like a seamstress guiding a silk hem under a sewing needle, she slid the paper in front of me.

"Please check box." Ji hee tapped her fingernail, painted Hawaiian Punch Pink. She touched the glittery velvet bow on her black headband. She seemed half human, half Minnie Mouse. "Please check," she repeated. I held the pen in my veiny hand. Ji hee seemed born for the girly things that left me bewildered. Like knowing which hair style flattered her face shape and what color blouse brought out her eyes. I, on the other hand, begrudged carrying a purse. Resented having to shave my knees. Compared with Ji hee, my X chromosome was half-baked.

I read the long menu of gynecological options; prices included. The list of procedures started out simple enough. Pap test 40,000 Korean Won (about 40 bucks); Prenatal screening

50,000 Won. Mammography 70,000 Won. They grew increasingly ominous -- Ovarian Cancer Marker, for example. Viral Load Test HIV. Some procedures raised questions. Perineal Reconstruction. Vaginal Wet Mount. Rectocele. *Who would elect to have their Recto celed?*

I checked the box in front of Pap test. Should I have also checked mammography? Blood tests?

Dr. Cheong's nurse ushered me down a stucco corridor and into a room stuffed with dated office furniture. On a black-smudged desktop stood a dusty rubberized model of a cervix and fallopian tubes. When it came to maintenance, South Korea stood spread eagled between high technology and low expectation. In my college classroom, with the tap of a computer icon, a projector lit up and a screen rolled down. Each morning I entered the room to find desktops cluttered with crumpled chip bags and candy wrappers. On the floor, lay empty plastic juice containers, tangled strands of black hair. I'd stand at the lectern, looking out at my students' flawlessly maintained faces juxtaposed with the unkempt condition of our room. *How curious*, I'd think.

"Put on these," the nurse said cheerfully, handing me a light stack of paper examination wear -- a wide pleated skirt and slippers in sanitation-worker blue.

"Thank you." I checked her nameplate -- *Seo-hyeon*.

I stepped behind the white curtained privacy screen located in the corner of the exam room and changed into my paper clothes. No height and weight check. No blood pressure measure. No peeing in a Dixie Cup. Strip from the waist down and don the disposable slippers. *Just the vagina, Ma'am.*

"Okay," Seo-hyeon said. "Come." She led me to the examination "table," which was more like a leather La-Z-Boy with stirrups. The examination recliner was lined with heavy white paper that crackled when I swung my legs up onto the thigh stirrups. I tucked the skirt pleats between my legs and waited for Dr. Cheong. My first gynecological exam in Seoul brought with it a few practical concerns. Would the doctor's English be proficient enough to explain any medical findings or issues? Would my Korean health insurance cover most of the fees? Where would I get my prescriptions filled? Did my body parts look just like theirs?

Dr. Cheong glanced at my paperwork. "Good afternoon, Woodford." Her shoulder-length black hair, shiny and steam pressed in place, curled up a bit at the collar of her lab coat. Her face was creaseless, baby powder white and moist-looking, as if she'd applied a microscopic layer of Crisco under her cream foundation.

With her delicate latex-gloved hands, Dr. Cheong lifted my paper skirt. "There will be a little pressure." Speculum inserted. "First, we do Pap test..." She swabbed, then placed the specimen collector into the vial to be sent to the laboratory. "Now we will look with sonogram." Sonogram? That surprised me. I hadn't checked that box. Perhaps sonograms were thrown in with the annual exam. She pointed to a 36-inch flat TV screen mounted to the wall in front of the exam recliner and inserted the sonogram probe. My insides flashed on the large screen monitor -- gray blurred images of my uterine wall. Dr. Cheong rotated the probe. "Tissue look healthy." There's my cervix...looked clear...Oh, and that pesky fibroid...no big deal...

Dr. Cheong cleared her throat. "No find ovary," she said. "I look...looking..." She angled the probe. "No, do not see."

You can't *find* my ovaries? *What do you mean? They're not car keys!*

"I don't understand," I said.

"As a woman age, ovary shrink," Dr. Cheong explained. "With time, ovary shrivel." I thought about other things that shriveled. A birthday balloon leaking air. My toes in the bathtub. A cold testicle.

Dr. Cheong pointed to the image on the screen. "Your ovary shrivel. This means you are most likely in menopause."

"Menopause?" My feet went cold inside my paper slippers. "But I'm not even fifty..." Like that would talk Dr. Cheong out of her diagnosis.

"We will check your hormone level to be sure," she said, "but, yes, menopause."

In South Korea, when a baby is born it is considered one year old. From a Korean perspective, I wasn't forty-nine-years-old. I was fifty. I'd passed a milestone birthday unaware. No Over-the-Hill T-shirt. No getting schnockered with friends. No quiet weekend reflecting on my first half-century of life. Where had it gone?

Dr. Cheong stood beside me. "Any questions, Woodford?"

Menopause. Does this mean time is running out? "Will I have hot flashes soon?"

"No worry." Dr. Cheong patted my shoulder with her gloved hand. *Was that the same hand that was just up my...?* Dr. Cheong was a woman of few words. Probably because she had few words, in English at least. It made her seem strong, like the silent cowboy smoking Marlboros and birthing calves out on the prairie. "Get dressed then come to office."

In her office, Dr. Cheong sat behind a heavy oak desk. Her framed degrees and awards were tacked on the wall behind her. Usuhan University. Society for Reproductive Medicine. International Board of Cosmetic Surgery.

I expected her to show me research regarding the pros and cons of hormone replacement therapy. Or point to a plastic model of a uterus with teeny ovaries. Instead, although my weight was within a healthy range for my height and body type, Dr. Cheong focused on fat levels. Waving the results of her own body mass tests, she advised, "You want chart to look like mine." She eyed me. "Next time you come here, I order body fat test for you and we see."

"Okay. But, uh, menopause…"

"I exercise there." She pointed to the corner of her office then sprang to her feet. "I have no time for gym, so jog in place and do…" She raised her arms up and down. Simultaneously bent at the waist. She moved like a marmoset on crack. "This is why my chart show weight very low, muscle very high, fat very low."

"Good for you…"

She sat down then looked at me. "All women get hormone therapy when your age," she said. "With no hormone, women look androgynous." She pointed to her upper lip. "Hair on face." Then moved her hands to her flat stomach. "Fat in middle." She shook her head. "Fat middle is man shape."

Dr. Cheong straightened her lab coat. "Now we talk about bone health, ek cetera." She talked about Calcium supplements and routine mammograms. Pointed to research indicating an increased risk of breast cancer, yet decreased risk of heart disease for women on hormone replacement. She sounded like a physician again.

"Question?" Dr. Cheong asked.

When will my hair start falling out? Does my insurance cover adult diapers? Will I ever love again? "Um, no."

"Good. Now I suggest cosmetic option for wrinkles." She squinted at my face. "Botox, I think."

*

Hot flashes. I stood on Seoul Subway's Line 2, shoulder-to-shoulder with commuters. It was winter. Sweat ran down the small of my back. Dripped from behind my ears. Trickled along my neck. I exited at Chungmuro station and walked a few blocks to Olive Young, a Korean Health and Beauty store. In South Korea, fastidious skin care seemed a cultural norm. The average Korean covered herself like a nuclear power plant worker when outdoors for any length of time. Most wore long sleeved shirts. High-wristed gloves. Brimmed hats with nylon face masks. The goal? To be white and smooth as the skin of a soft-boiled egg.

I was an outdoorsy person from Rochester, New York. My skin had been blasted for decades by ice pellets, burned and blistered by mid-July rays. Because who bothers to wear sunblock in *Rochester*?

The doors at Olive Young swushed open and I stepped inside. My face flushed. *It feels like a hundred degrees in this place.* I tugged at my sweatshirt. Sweat pooled in my cleavage and dribbled down the backs of my legs. *A fucking inferno!* The other patrons in the store wore winter coats, wool slacks, scarves. Underneath my sweatshirt, I was wearing a ratty gray tank top. Sweat dripped from the nape of my neck, along my temples. I peeled off my sweatshirt, stuffed it in my Olive Young hand basket. My skin was flaky, spotted, and blotchy. I slunk through the store looking like a hairless cat with eczema.

The salesclerks spotted me. In me they'd met their fantasy client. A chance to put their aesthetician license to proper use in an otherwise routine day of scanning barcodes and re-stocking tampons on aisle 6B. They went all crazy-eyed and wet-lipped. Approached me with pink containers filled with moisturizers, whitening creams and anti-wrinkle lotions. *We make you look young!* they promised. I was there to buy cotton swabs and Chapstick.

That night I called my mother. It was nine o'clock in Seoul. New York was thirteen hours behind. My mother's a morning person. "Good morning, Mom. How's your week going?"

My mother and stepfather, Stan, still lived in the small town in which I grew up, thirty miles south of Rochester. Stan and my mother married when I was six years old, soon after my parents' divorce. They were elderly now, in their seventies, yet my mind's eye often recollected them as forty-somethings -- brunette and able-bodied – lobbing tennis balls over the net in our town park court or jitterbugging in the living room on New Year's Eve.

"Everything's fine here," my mother said. Last Tuesday, she'd had a follow-up with her primary care physician, Dr. Henderson, about her hypertension. This Friday she'd take Stan to the orthopedist to check on that knee of his. She put a happy spin on things. "On our way home from Dr. Henderson's last week, we had lunch at Applebee's." They'd made a day of it. Post-appointment Fiesta Chicken and Double Crunch Shrimp.

I didn't mention my hot flashes, kept the conversation I'd had with Dr. Cheong to myself. A few years back, I'd brought up the topic of menopause with my mother. "End of an era" was her synopsis of the experience, a phrase she often used in conjunction with "over and done with." Perhaps, for my mother, "end of an era" seemed a more concrete, less messy, way of processing transition. "End of an era" was also my mother's code for giving up stuff she claimed to have limited passion for in the first place. Like having everyone over to her house for Thanksgiving dinner, buying Christmas gifts for adult children. Like Sex.

For me, however, my mother's articulation of life stages defined with such finality only served to conjure more questions. Where were the blurry edges? Where was the notion of passage? The time to feel the bitter sweetness of grief for what was no longer possible then open ourselves, with curiosity and awe, to what might lie ahead for our bodies, hearts, souls?

Winter had taken hold of New York. Frigid and grim-faced. I turned the topic to plans for springtime. Asked what she and Stan planned to plant in their garden come May. Gardening was a favorite hobby. Their dinner conversations often centered around frost predictions, sun exposure for cherry tomatoes, pros and cons for summer squash versus zucchini.

"Oh, that's over and done with," my mother said. "Stan finally sold the tiller." She talked about Stan's recent heart valve stent. Her arthritic joints.

But you love to garden, I reminded her. There's nothing like fresh tomatoes from the vine. And everyone loves your zucchini bread...

"Who needs it?" my mother said. "That's what grocery stores are for."

At times, it seemed my mother longed for things she'd given up. Like her years of working as a registered nurse when she checked IV's, monitored blood pressure, applied antibiotic ointment and gauze. The "white tornado," her colleagues called her, since she strode down medical corridors – in her pressed, white uniform and nurse's cap – at a fast, efficient clip. Since her retirement, my mother's emails had read more like medical notes. Talking about her morning *prep* and returning a phone call *stat.* When I visit my mother nowadays – hunched forward, clunking her cane against the pavement – I'm initially taken aback. Her petite, marshmallowy frame looks familiar, her pretty hands, her Nordic, blush cheeks. Her skin is soft and delicate as I remember and her wispy, fine hair frames her face like before. Yet, for a moment, I'm bewildered. *Where's the white tornado?*

I held the phone close to my ear. Not even a small garden? I nudged.

"Those days are over," my mother said. "You know. End of an era."

I wondered what seeds my mother might sow now that her gardening days were over. Over the course of her adult life, she'd seemed content to focus on taking care of others. She'd raised her three children, doted over Stan, took care of her patients at the nursing home. I, on the other hand, at this time in my life, felt less clarity of purpose.

*

Dr. Cheong sent my test results: POSITIVE FOR MENOPAUSE.

Dear Woodford

The test results show that you are in menopause.

Although you may still have some occasional periods.

Other hormones are ok.

I hope to see you soon for further management.

Best regards,

Eun Sook Cheong, MD.

I phoned the clinic to schedule an appointment for Dr. Cheong to manage my menopause. Was it possible, I asked, to see the doctor in the next couple of weeks?

"Is tomorrow okay?" was the receptionist's response. "Nine o'clock?"

How do they do it? In Seoul, thriving medical and dental practices seemed capable of fitting me into their schedules on practically a moment's notice.

In Rochester, to schedule an appointment with my gynecologist, I needed to call months in advance unless I was in the midst of a gynecological crisis. Like my uterus falling onto the bathroom floor while brushing my teeth or discovering that one of my holes had closed up. When I called the Rochester office to schedule a pap smear, I'd get, "Ooh, that's gonna run you three months out." The clerk would add, "We're booking into October for routine appointments."

What if I throw in a mammogram? I'd press. It's been a while.

"Do you have a lump or foul-smelling discharge?"

No.

"Sorry." She'd stifle a yawn. "How's October twenty-first?"

A mere twenty-four hours after my telephone conversation with Dr. Cheong's receptionist, I was sitting in their waiting room beside an end table piled with Botox and Collagen brochures.

Seo-hyeon ushered me into the doctor's office. "Hello, Woodford," Dr. Cheong said. She propped her elbows on the desktop, resting her chin on intertwined fingers. She leaned toward me, smiling with gentle eyes.

"Good morning." On her bookshelf, stood a framed family photograph of a beaming Dr. Cheong with grown children and, *Was that a grandchild?*

Dr. Cheong leaned back and leafed through my medical file. "This is follow-up visit," she clarified.

"Yes." To prevent the conversation from pivoting from gynecology to cosmetic options for my middle-aged face, I quickly added, "We talked about hormone replacement therapy…"

"I consider options for you, Woodford." Dr. Cheong slid a packet of paper toward me. Lists of medications and side effects. Well-woman screening guidelines. Laboratory testing and evaluation recommendations. "I want you to be healthy and comfortable, have good bone health and heart health…"

Dr. Cheong and I discussed my changing body. Talked about clinical trials. Prescription dosage. Prevention of osteoporosis. She seemed like a professional who cared, who understood. Was she a woman who'd also reached the end of an era? Who, like myself, wondered how many good years she had left? Maybe only twenty. Or thirty. Like me, did she wonder: If youth could be lost, what could be found? It was as if my new life in South Korea, in this land of wrinkle-free beauties, was tapping my shoulder. Dr. Cheong's confirmation of menopause had gotten my attention. I was a middle-aged woman rather than a youthful one. Time for me to reach forward rather than grasp back for what was. I was entering into a new season. Rather than grim winter, could I feel the awe of spring?

"Thank you, Dr. Cheong." I stood, pushed in my chair, stepped outside her office. In the corridor, a young nurse whirred by. She wore a pressed white uniform. A stethoscope hung around her neck, its silver end rhythmically tapping against her chest like a heartbeat thumping. Steadily. Predictably. As if the end of an era wasn't just around the corner.

PROSPECTS

There was a time, well before arriving in Korea, that I was married to a kind and gentle man. Our legal separation was the most amiable in the universe, friends told me. Sixteen years into our twenty-year marriage, I'd begun agonizing over the split -- which I knew in my heart, mind and soul needed to come to fruition -- before filing the papers. I hadn't known, at the age of twenty-three when I married, what I'd need in a partner at the age of forty-three. It felt to me like our marriage had wasted away slowly. For two decades, the heart of our marital relationship seemed to beat at one pace -- slow, measured. And at one volume – hushed, reserved. Until flatlined.

Now single and living in Asia, I enthusiastically anticipated romantic prospects. In Korea, I'd be an exotic foreigner. A woman of the world. What hot, Asian guy could resist that? I'd possess automatic charm power. Like the Brit at a house party in Deerfield, Kansas spinning tales about drinking Guinness with Prince Harry at a neighborhood pub in the town of Happy Bottom. In Korea, I'd be the Mary Tyler Moore of Seoul. Strolling confidently down city sidewalks, smiling skyward, taking the town. I'd get chatted up by handsome Korean businessmen. Asked out by American or Irish or Australian men. Adventurous expats resembling hot *CNN* journalists in khaki pants with lots of pockets.

South Korea, with its population of 50 million, includes approximately 22,000 foreign English teachers. Half of those foreigners are women, leaving 11,000 men, most of whom are twenty-somethings fresh out of college. Most Korean men my age spoke very little English. The few Western men over the age of forty seemed to be into Asian women. In terms of sheer numbers of potential romantic partners, I was screwed. Or most likely, not.

In Seoul, I sat cross-legged on the twin bed in my studio apartment taking on the tedious task of creating an online dating profile. What are you looking for in an ideal match? *A pulse and his own teeth.* I typed, "A gentleman who is kind, well-educated, healthy and engaged in life." What's your biggest pet peeve? *I'm not a fan of public bum scratching or babies who blat like donkeys.* "Chronic lateness," I wrote. What do you enjoy doing in your leisure time? *Talking to myself, eating Chips Ahoy by the bag, drinking beer through a straw.* "I enjoy hiking."

My dating profile indicated clearly that I lived in Korea. The next day, I received an email from Stanley in Poughkeepsie.

Good day, it read. *My name is Stanley. I am interested in buying your automobile for sale. Is it still in good condition? What is the final price? When can I come for an inspection? Kindly get back to me with more details. Warm Regards.* I considered playing with the euphemism. Asking Stanley what I might find under his chassis. Telling him my Cadillac needs an oil check. Might he know anyone with a good dip stick?

My message inbox flashed an electronic *wink* from Jeong-hun, a fifty-six-year-old business executive. *Ooh, executive.*

Would I like to meet for dinner at the Ritz Carlton? He had a gym membership at the Ritz and could take his workout before dinner. *Mmm, all pumped up.* Would Saturday work? We'd meet at the first-floor restaurant. Their Jeju-style pork and scallion pancakes were quite good.

The day before my date with Jeong-hun, I stood in my bra and panties facing the bathroom mirror. Stared quizzically at folds of flab oozing beneath my elastic straps and above my waist band. *Who turned on the lava machine?*

I walked five blocks to my neighborhood jimjilbang -- Korean public bath. If I couldn't be buff, I could at least be clean. The jimjilbang receptionist tapped the number 8,000 on her calculator pad, slid it toward me. 8,000 Korean Won. About eight U.S. dollars. She handed me a locker key. Two body towels the size of dish rags. Baggy pajama shorts and matching T-shirt for the casual dining area where men and women congregated after their baths to eat gimbap and kimchijeon, play a quick game of ping-pong.

In the Ladies' locker room, a large-screen television showing Disney's *Aladdin* dubbed in Korean was mounted high on a wall. It faced vinyl-padded lounging islands where naked Korean women and girls stretched out. Bodies still, eyes half closed. Sunning iguanas. Nearby was a sales counter. Pink razors, yellow scrubbing mitts, packets of mung bean facial masks on display. "Annyeong Haseyo," I said, placing a mitt and mask on the countertop. My Korean was minimal. This salesclerk had no calculator. Like a child, I held out a fan of Korean Won. I preferred purchasing my shower supplies before undressing for the baths. Three older Korean women beside me at the counter stood buck naked. Their bare breasts flapped against the countertop when reaching for shampoo packets and body lotions. Mammary windsocks.

"Annyeong Haseyo," the salesclerk replied. Middle-aged and thickset, the clerk wore only a black bra, panties, shower shoes. Jimjilbang workers rotated posts. She was on sales counter duty right then. Later, she might be cleaning Jacuzzis or abrading a patron with sea salts in the hot, steamy bath area. Underwear-for-work made sense. I placed my left hand beneath my right forearm – a Korean gesture of politeness. The clerk gingerly plucked four bills from my hand, placed a Korean coin in my palm. She flashed the tender smile one gives to the unknowing and dear and, most likely, mentally challenged.

Clutching a towel to my bare chest, I swung open the glass door to the bath area. Jimjilbang Cardinal Rule: *Be clean, aseptic as a surgical probe before you even think about dipping your bare ass in the communal baths.* I squatted on a low plastic stool at a shower station equipped with a faucet, mobile shower head and cruel, mocking mirror. I soaped, lathered, and loofah-scrubbed. Everything. Raw.

So many baths. Hot Jacuzzies. Cold Jacuzzies. Foot hydrotherapy spas. Herbally-treated tubs. In a cavernous, tiled room, about forty Korean women and I shuffled our wet bodies from tub to tub. I stepped into a steaming hot herbal bath, standing thigh-high in pea-soup green water. I dipped my bottom beneath the surface, raised it out quickly. Dip and rise, dip and rise. Like the cartoon I once saw of Bugs Bunny easing into a scalding bath, his buttocks red as a branding iron. I acclimated, sunk shoulder-deep, rested the nape of my neck against the ceramic Jacuzzi wall. My legs floated, my knees and toes peeking pale through murky waters. I breathed out, savoring a few moments of calm on my journey through unchartered territory.

In the lobby of the Ritz Carlton, my stacked heels clicked on the marble floor. I ducked into the restroom. Re-dabbed my pink lipstick -- Mature Rose. At the restaurant, the hostess bowed. I surveyed the room of Korean men seated at tables clothed in white linen. Navy suits. Pressed shirts. Jeong-hun stood then grinned warmly and slowly nodded, like a good-hearted monk. *Only hotter.*

"It is a privilege to meet you," he said, clasping my hands in his. *Strong fingers.* Jeong-hun smoothed his charcoal black hair. His eyes were the color of hickory, framed in long lashes, and creaseless -- what Koreans called "single-lid." They shined when he smiled. We chatted about last week's cold spell, the Ritz's beautiful marble lobby, and the amazing restaurants in Seoul. Then Jeong-hun told me about his supervisory work in an electronics department at Samsung. He talked about liquid crystal displays. Thin film Transistors. Active-matrix organic light-emitting diodes. His English was perfect, but I didn't understand a word. He asked about the classes I teach. About my former life in New York. Whether I was enjoying Seoul. He was nice, so pleasant. Exactly what my dating profile claimed I was looking for. *A gentleman who is kind, well-educated, healthy and engaged in life.* We sipped hot, dandelion tea. Pinched Jeju-style pork with sterling silver chopsticks. "Dinner again next week, please?" Jeong-hun asked. He'd take me to a fine restaurant in Apgujeong. Their Jungsik salad and crispy duck were excellent.

I was raised in a rural environment in upstate New York. Where men worked the land or at least mowed the lawn with a hand mower. They had calloused palms, chins with coarse whiskers. Their ear hair grew in tufts. During pubescence, those images of manhood entered my sexual psyche.

Korean men tended to be clean shaven with mousse-styled hair. Most had chiseled noses, hairless forearms, and chests. To me, they looked smooth as newborn kittens. My female colleagues loved that about Korean men. Ooh! They're like Olympic swimmers, they said.

Before moving to Asia, I'd seen images of Korean men. I found their lean bodies and black hair appealing, considered them handsome. I understood that, in general, their physical appearance was not necessarily what I considered "my type." But as a woman traveling the world, I'd assumed I'd be more versatile, embrace the global community in every aspect. Sitting here with Jeong-hun, I was faced with the contrast between recognizing attractiveness and feeling attracted.

Sexual chemistry, for me, was multi-faceted. Perhaps the lack of zing I felt toward Jeong-hun had to do with our conversation feeling informative and polite rather than connective. But I couldn't deny the lack of luster I felt toward him physically. I realized I preferred visibly brimming testosterone. Protruding Adam's Apples, hairy knuckles, a one o'clock shadow. I once dated a man so furry that if you entered a ski lodge to find him lying naked on his belly in front of the fireplace, you'd mistake him for a bear skin rug. Sign me up!

Jeong-hun was an accomplished, attractive man and the last thing I wanted to do was waste his time by leading him on in the face of my uncertainty. Placing my hand on Jeong-hun's hairless wrist, I said, "It was a privilege to meet you. You are such a nice gentleman, but...I'm sorry."

"No worries," Jeong-hun assured me, bringing a piece of pork to his lips. "There are many bright fish in the ocean."

A MILD INCONVENIENCE

My supervisor at Wangja University showed up in the lobby of our on-campus apartment building. "You must leave campus in five days," Dr. Sung told me. There was a temporary faculty housing shortage. He mentioned something about prestigious mathematicians from Sweden or Milwaukee visiting campus for a while. Researching non-Euclidian geometries, perhaps, or studying the number 3.

Dr. Sung continued, "You move into a new apartment. Stay for eight weeks. Then move back." He smiled. "Okay?"

Well, this sucks. I liked my fifth-floor apartment at Wangja. It was modern, clean, compact. Its large, square window overlooked student dormitories and the campus 7-Eleven. It was a nano flat with a view. And my morning commute to work was a one-minute walk to the building next door. Dr. Sung shook my hand. "Thank you for your understanding," he said. "Now pack."

When I'd relocated to Korea, I'd crammed necessities into one jumbo suitcase, a small carry-on and backpack. I'd packed for four seasons in sets of two. Brown and black woven winter slacks. White linen and khaki pants. Two navy skirts. Two pair of jeans. Black shorts and beige shorts. Cardigan sweaters and silky blouses. Sandals and black pumps. Sneakers and hiking boots. A Noah's Ark of work and leisure attire.

I lugged and rolled my Ark to the new apartment, located a fifteen-minute walk off-campus. The four-story cement building was situated between a construction dumpster and tire store. The building was being renovated. Saw dust and drywall flakes clung to radiators and flooring, like dandruff on the shoulders of a dark blue suit.

My new second-floor apartment, half the size of my Wangja studio, had a knee-high bed with thin mattress. It was like a kiddie bed with added leg room. No television. No internet connection. Its small window overlooked a side street where a gray cat sniffed garbage scraps and an old guy pushed a bicycle through a muddy gulley.

When I talked with friends and relatives, they referred to my life overseas as an adventure. "Guess this is part of the adventure," I mumbled, removing slacks and a blouse from my suitcase. I ironed them in preparation for work the next morning. Unwrapped soap for the shower. Set my shoes and sneakers near the doorway. Taped newspaper to the lower windowpane for privacy.

Accepting the reality that this was my new home for the next two months, I settled into routine. Teaching English classes during the day, cooking and reading in the evening. Jogging along the Hangang River in the morning. Writing in my journal before bedtime. Finding myself in an apartment with no internet connection, I checked emails at work, stopped looking at dating sites, and my internal boil to meet a man calmed to a simmer. Maybe my date with Jeong-hun had helped me face the reality that finding romance here would take time. Or perhaps I was relaxing into the ease of solitude. Either way, I was pleased with my good attitude.

Around that time and unbeknownst to me, back home in New York, a 60-foot section of tree fell on my father. He was seventy-three years old, at the time, and harvesting timber for firewood with his neighbor, Keith. The hardwood leaned at an unpredicted angle placing my father in the drop zone, fracturing his left shoulder, and cracking his skull wide open. "So much blood," his neighbor would eventually tell me. Keith fished my father's cell phone from the back pocket of his bloodied jeans and jabbed 9-1-1 with trembling hands. Mercy Flight skids touched down on field grass. Medics rushed the woods with a stretcher, hemostatic dressing, trauma scissors. Mercy carried my father, unconscious, at a clip of 120 mph to the rooftop of Strong Memorial Hospital where it alighted on a helipad, its rotor blades whirring in whispers, *Will he make it?*

Sunday afternoon, I scouted my Seoul neighborhood for a PC bang – internet cafe – and found one tucked between a used textbook vendor and electronics shop. A sign outside the building read -- Internet Monkey! – and featured a graphic of a fluorescent green chimp smiling at a computer screen, its fingers wrapped around a joystick.

I descended the stairs to the PC bang -- a large, windowless room reeking of cigarette smoke and filled with oily-haired teens in headphones playing video games -- and caught the attention of a twenty-something in black hoodie who sat slumped behind the reception desk. He gestured for me to sit at any unoccupied computer, so I slid into the first chair I saw that wasn't strewn with candy wrappers or cookie crumbs and logged in to check emails.

My friend, Tina, had emailed. She'd watched a movie that was set in South Korea. Said the lead actor was hot. Asked if I knew that Koreans cut their beef with scissors. *I did.* My mother had written. Had I heard that Cousin Lester was moving to Florida? *I hadn't.* She was taking Stan to the doctor to have a benign cyst removed, she added. And attached a cute photo of her cat, Bella, drinking running water from the tap.

My father hadn't replied to my last email. *Huh.* My father lived in a rural community and owned a hundred acres or so of land. His farmhouse wasn't wired for internet, so he checked emails once a week at the town library, usually on Tuesdays. He would have seen the email I'd sent last week. If I were back in New York, I'd simply pick up the phone. Check in on my elderly father who lived by himself surrounded by acres of pasture and woods. With days and nights being flipped between Korea and the U.S., I composed a new email. Subject line: What's new?

Back in my apartment, I sat with a cup of tea, reminding myself that time often seemed to get away from my father. For decades, he'd balanced his career as full professor while maintaining a horse farm and correspondence was, at times, sporadic. A few years ago, when asked about his transition from employee to retiree, he'd joked, "Retirement isn't for wusses." He'd purchased additional acreage, built a new barn, thrown himself into volunteer work in the community. While he and I emailed regularly, it wasn't all that unusual not to hear back for a while. He'd probably aborted his library visit to hog brush a field or dig fence post holes. There was always some project that he needed to tend to. Small farm urgent care.

That night, I awoke at 3:12 a.m. feeling restless with concern. Being 2:12 p.m. in New York, I called my father. His phone rang and rang, then:

Beep. Sorry I missed your call. When you leave a message, please speak slowly and loudly. My hearing's not very good at all. Thank you. Beep.

"Hi, Dad. Just calling to see how you're doing. Everything's fine here in Korea. Haven't heard from you in a while. Shoot me an email when you get a chance. Love you."

My teaching schedule here in Seoul was steadfast. Monday through Friday, I arrived at my desk at 8:30 a.m., started teaching at 9:00 a.m., stopped teaching at 5:00 p.m. and stayed for office hours on Mondays, Tuesdays, and Thursdays until 6:30 p.m.

On Friday, I was told that I needed to wrap up my English Conversation class at 4:00 p.m. instead of 5:00 p.m. so my students could attend some required on-campus program. *Great! An early start to the weekend.* I returned home from work at 4:20 p.m., tapped my security code into the apartment's keypad and opened the door.

Half the contents of my small refrigerator had been emptied onto the floor. It took a moment for this to register. My bag of lettuce, container of leftover pasta, yellow peppers, jar of salsa, wrapped block of cheese, packet of chicken breasts, and bag of mushrooms lay heaped on the floor.

My refrigerator door was propped open with a black metal lunch box and thermos bottle. The kind you see at construction sites. Two Korean men in work clothes squatted near the fridge, eating hard boiled eggs and kimchi out of plastic containers. Two women – wives, perhaps, or girlfriends – squatted nearby, shoveling rice into their mouths with chopsticks. I stepped inside the apartment. Glanced at the open refrigerator. It was filled with the workmen's food. Plastic tubs of kimchi and red chili paste. Bags of hard-boiled eggs. Jars of juice. A rotisserie chicken. A cabbage head. "Sorry, sorry," one of the workmen said, then flapped his hands, gesturing to the others – *Foreign Lady came home early. Let's get the hell out of here!*

Apparently, while I was at work all day, the workers used my apartment as their employee lounge. *That explains why my apartment smelled like fermented cabbage and cooked egg yolk.* How many days had they been doing this? Picnicking in my all-in-one living space -- kitchen, living room, bedroom. Had they pointed and laughed at my damp sports bra hung on the doorknob? At my orthodontic retainer on the sink? At the Milky Way wrappers on the countertop? At the little, pink vibrator beneath my kiddie bed?

I stood motionless. The women and workmen scurried. Removed their items from the refrigerator. Stuffed them into shopping bags.

One of the men reached toward the piles of my food, about to return them to the refrigerator. "It's okay," I said, waving my hands. I stepped near my food and added, "Bye, Bye." They rushed toward the door, bowing and murmuring in Korean.

Kneeling on the floor, I gathered my food, returned perishable items to refrigerator shelves. My tiny apartment was not exactly cozy. It was aesthetically unimpressive, but it was my home, if only temporarily. It served as a warm place to curl up and read a book, a refuge from busy city streets, a private space for me to eat, sleep, shower. Or so I'd thought. In one afternoon, a couple of workmen with a master key, thermoses and a big bag of hard-boiled eggs had rocked my sense of security, of safekeeping.

The rain fell in torrents that evening, but I walked to Internet Monkey! anyway, rushing between awnings, my sneakers squishing, saturated. Most computers were occupied by teens virtually directing action figures in black armor to high kick, low crawl, or blow things up. I sat at a computer and logged in, feeling static with nerves. Still no email from my father.

Walking back to my apartment, fat raindrops glowed iridescent under streetlamps. I walked slowly, already soaked, water streaming beneath my feet. When I arrived at my apartment, I stripped off wet clothes, piled them into a heap at the door.

It was eight o'clock in Seoul, making it seven o'clock in the morning in New York. I called my father.

Ring…Ring…Ring…

"Dad? Hi! How are you?"

Well, I'm doing just fine now.

"Now?"

The doctors say I'm recovering at record speed.

"What?"

A tree fell on me.

"Huh?"

A tree. Keith and I were cutting oak for firewood…Doctor Turlington came to my hospital room the morning after the accident. He said, 'I knew you'd make it.'

"That's good…uh, I guess…"

Then Dr. Turlington said, 'But I was the only one in this hospital who thought so.'

The levity I initially felt from hearing my father's voice took on water as I learned details about the gravity of his accident. He'd been unconscious for six hours. Had no recollection of the Mercy flight. He'd suffered a severe skull fracture requiring over thirty sutures, incurred subarachnoid bleeding, a subdural hematoma. His left shoulder had been dislocated and badly broken. After his discharge from the hospital, his second ex-wife drove eight hours to care for him. She stayed at his house for four days. He remembered nearly nothing of the visit. But it was true, what he told me from the onset of our conversation. My father was recovering at record speed.

By the time I moved back into my studio apartment at Wangja University, my father had completed hours of physical therapy and resumed his daily work on his farm.

In the lobby of my on-campus apartment building, Dr. Sung greeted me. "Your key," he said, smiling broadly. "Welcome back."

"Thank you," I said, bowing slightly.

"Thank *you*," Dr. Sung replied. "For enduring a mild inconvenience."

Later that day, after transporting my Ark of packed clothing back to my apartment and hauling my backpack, bags of groceries, boxes of toiletries and odds and ends from the temporary housing to my on-campus studio, I chuckled at Dr. Sung's description – "mild inconvenience."

Standing in front of my apartment window, watching students chatting and laughing as they scurried from their dormitories to the campus 7-Eleven, my eight weeks in that crappy little temporary apartment felt like a distant memory. I supposed that moving was simply part of my new norm. A mild inconvenience compared to, say, having a 60-foot section of tree fall on me.

But I sure was glad to be back in my nano-flat with internet connection, a TV and one-minute commute to work. And a view of people coming and going about their daily lives, buying

Shrimp Crackers, Choco Pies, and Café Benne to take back to their dormitories. All settled in their routines until something disrupted it. Like a failed Geometry quiz, an upsetting phone call from home, an argument with a girlfriend, or some other mild inconvenience.

More Complicated

Since arriving in South Korea, I'd welcomed the quiet that accompanied the language barrier, the background whir of incomprehensible-to-me Korean words. Built-in white noise. Stillness.

I could sit in a tea house in Hongdae reading a novel, uninterrupted by the dialogue around me since I had no clue what was being said. Back in New York, I'd get hooked in, distracted, by conversations at nearby café tables. Some guy complaining to his friend that his wife had dragged him through Hobby Lobby for two hours to shop for fabric and candles. Some sorority girl telling her sister that she "shaved her vagina" on date nights. I'd stare back down at my book. *What page was I on?*

Throughout the years, I'd participated in plenty of spiritual retreats. *Free yourself from the daily grind. Retreat into silence.* Daily meditation. Chanting. Prayerful walks in the forest. During those retreats, I bonded with the women in my dormitory room. We sat on our bunks in T-shirts and Indian pants, jotting in journals, reading Thich Nhat Hanh. Some of my bunkmates had lip or eyebrow piercings, others had tattooed shoulders. Most had B.O., but it didn't matter. We were all one.

Chuseok is a national holiday in which Koreans make a pilgrimage back to their hometowns. They eat rice cake and bibimbap with family members. Pay their respects to ancestors. Some wear traditional Hanbok – ankle-length flared dresses for women, and long-sleeved boxy vests and trousers for men. They bring their family hosts time-honored food gifts like cow bone and ginseng. For Koreans, Chuseok meant holding memorial services for their forebearers. For me, it meant a four-day weekend.

For part of that weekend, I signed up for a Buddhist temple stay. Two days of peaceful contemplation. An opportunity to quiet my mind, reflect on my life purpose, try to understand what I was yearning for, what might be missing in my life that prompted my travels to begin with, my search.

*

"You must hurry!" A temple staff person motioned for me to follow him. I was late. I'd underestimated the length of my subway ride from my apartment to Hananim Temple even though I'd carefully researched the route. Line 4 to Dongmyo. Line 6 to Taereung then to Line 7. Depart at Suraksan station. Hop a local bus. Walk half a mile to the temple. With holiday travelers, the metro was busier than usual. I'd been unable to squeeze onto overly crowded trains and forced to wait for the next to pull up. By the time I stepped off the local bus and jogged, my backpack bouncing, the half mile to the temple, I was already fifteen minutes late.

I rushed up the hill towards the 1,000-year-old spiritual compound. I'd been told to meet at the temple pavilion. I could see it in the distance, its black ceramic-tiled rooftop curved up into a gentle smile. I ran past the dharma and disciples' halls. Past the gold-painted, wooden Buddha statues. Past the meditation room.

I was one of a dozen temple stay participants that weekend. Nine Koreans. Three American expats. When I arrived, the eleven others were standing outside the temple dressed in baggy, gray linen pants and boxy yellow vests. They were waiting for the monk. "You late!" a woman called out. The staff person, Sang-ook, ushered me toward a wooden staircase.

"Hurry!" he said. When we reached the second floor, Sang-ook slipped off his sandals and pointed at my feet. "No shoe." I bent to untie my sneakers. "Must not keep monk waiting!" He dashed to the end of the hallway. Rummaged through a stack of temple wear, glancing at my body to assess my size. He handed me a pair of drawstring pants and a vest to be worn over my T-shirt then flapped his hands toward a nearby changing room. I darted into it, pulled the vest on over my T-shirt. Whisked off my shorts and slipped on the pants. They were huge. *Does he really think my ass is this big?* I tightened the drawstring around my waist and stepped from the room. "Follow," Sang-ook said. He disappeared down the stairs.

Once outdoors, we approached the monk. He was a stocky, kind-faced gentleman dressed in an ankle-length gray robe, the color of a cloud contemplating rain. "Bow!" Sang-ook instructed. "Monk very important man."

The monk led our group to the perimeter of the complex, his robe swishing as he walked along the pine-needle-lined path to a gazebo nestled between camellias and trees. The monk stood quietly for a moment, his shaven scalp glistening in the heat, his ears hugging close to the sides of his sun-kissed head. He spoke only Korean, but Myung-hee, a temple staff member, was there to translate. "Where did you come from?" he asked us. Our circle of participants took turns answering -- Daejeon. Gwangju. Los Angeles. Uljin.

Based on past retreats, I figured there was a more spiritually evolved response. Something along the lines of, *I've come from nowhere. I've always been.* Clearing my throat, I said, "Upstate New York."

The monk spoke, pausing to breathe deeply while gazing at the trees, speaking in gentle whirring sounds of "ahs" and "ohs." *Where did you come from?* The Korean participants listened attentively. Nodding. Their eyes slightly squinted in thoughtful consideration of the monk's message. He talked on – "Dangxineun dangxinboda horicin du dangsin yuctewa gaseong…" And on. Several minutes later, the monk stopped talking. He clasped his hands in front of his belly, exhaled a gentle sigh. Then nodded at Myung-hee.

Myung-hee faced us three native English speakers. She interpreted simply, "No, you come from different place. More complicate."

Years ago, I attended a spiritual retreat at an abbey led by a Cistercian monk -- Brother Doyle. There, monastics lived a simple life of prayer and contemplation, theological study, and service. Silence was observed at the Abbey, speaking in a limited way, only when necessary. "The no talking rule is really not complicated," Brother Doyle instructed us. "Unless there's an emergency, you keep it zipped."

During that week I'd sentenced myself to seven days of silent reflection in a stuffy, second-floor room with a twin bed, lamp, and desk the size of a tray table. Brother Doyle led an optional, hour-long colloquy. I'd skipped the first one, afraid of discussing theological questions with a Roman Catholic monastic. I wasn't Catholic. Or Protestant. Or Jewish. Or anything. I was Unsettled.

Two and a half days later, after pacing my room and eating stewed vegetables in silence, I secretly hoped for a kitchen fire. Just a minor one. *You turn off the burners,* I'd tell the cook. *I'll get the fire extinguisher.* I could get a good ten spoken words out of that one. Another day passed. I saw a note posted on the bulletin board: Colloquy with Brother Doyle. 3:00pm to 4:00pm at the Retreat House Library. *Talking! Oh, boy!*

I arrived fifteen minutes early for the colloquy. A flabby-chested young man in his twenties was already there, seated in a cushioned chair near the built-in bookshelf with cut stone bookends in the shape of praying hands. The Abbey cook sat down, apron-less and smelling of Cumin. An elderly woman with wispy lavender-gray hair entered the room, her left hip rising higher than her right as she walked. She wore white orthopedic shoes. *From all those years of toe-curling sex?*

At three o'clock on the nose, Brother Doyle barreled in. "Greetings!" He plopped his body down in a padded swivel chair, wiped his sweaty palms on the black tunic overlaying his white robe. "It's a hot one. Phew!" He'd just returned from his outreach work, he explained, volunteering as a counselor in a neighboring community outside the Abbey. "Okay, what's on our minds today?" he began. "Let's talk."

The elderly woman wanted to know what kind of community work Brother Doyle did.

"I work with addicts," he said. "People addicted to drugs, sex and pornography."

She pressed a finger to her hearing aid. “Drugs and what else?”

“Sex and pornography,” Brother Doyle repeated.

That got the young man’s attention. “Cool,” he said.

Brother Doyle leaned forward and offered a gentle warning. “Don’t think for a minute that you and I are any different from the addicts I work with,” he said. “We’re all one. Each one of us has our addiction, our drug of choice that we reach for when faced with challenges.”

His addiction, he told us, was inhaling Lay’s Potato Chips by the bag. “If I have a bad day, there aren’t enough bags of potato chips in the world.” He looked at each of us with gray-blue eyes. “Maybe your addiction is beer,” he said. “Or Oxycodone. Or reefer. Or work. We all struggle, don’t we?” He paused. We nodded. “Jesus sees our struggles and He says to us, ‘Come home’.”

Brother Doyle went around the room, pointing to each of us, asking what came to our minds when hearing the word, *Home.* The elderly woman said, “Family.”

“A safe place to fall,” said the young guy.

“Love,” said the cook.

Brother Doyle turned toward me. *Home. That space between breaths? That moment of wonder at the sight of a seemingly endless winter sky?* “I’m drawing a blank,” I told him.

Brother Doyle offered an answer to his own question. “Freedom,” he said.

I stared at a faded coffee stain on the Berber carpet, the splotch’s edges irregular and blurred. “Freedom?” I asked, wanting to understand.

“There’s no right answer, but sit with it for a while,” Brother Doyle suggested. “Freedom.”

*

"Meet at big bell!" Sang-ook called to our group. "Meet at big bell!" We rushed to the pavilion that housed a five-foot-tall bronze bell with raised inscription and ornamentation. "Meditation. Follow me!"

We followed Sang-ook to the meditation hall. Climbed stairs to a stark white, brightly lit room on the third floor with a wall of small, square windows that were screenless and open. Each of us claimed a brown rectangular mat, lined up in three rows, on the blonde-wood floor.

Myung-hee, thin-shouldered with black hair pulled into a ponytail, sat facing us at the front of the room. Full lotus -- ankles propped atop opposite thighs, her shins, bent knees and feet forming a flattened X. "If you no do lotus," she said, glancing down at her legs, "it is okay." We could sit cross-legged, Myung-hee explained, but our eyes should remain fully open. "No sleepy," she reminded us. "Very important." We were instructed to sit still, quiet. Count our breaths, each inhale and exhale to ten, then repeat for fifty minutes. In the past, while meditating, I'd follow my breath or repeat a mantra, my eyes half-closed, trying to let thoughts pass by, like leaves floating in a stream, rather than grasping onto them. Allowing my eyelids to rest at half-mast while meditating did not generally create a sleep risk for me, but Myung-hee had instructed us to keep our eyes fully open, and I wanted to follow the monastery's protocol.

Settling in on my mat, I attempted to quiet my mind but felt distracted by the sight of the people seated in the row in front of me. I tried to stare straight ahead, but my eyes fixated on the twitching of the skinny, young man's shoulder blades then shifted to the middle-aged woman's wriggling toes. The air in the room felt hot and still. The sun had set, and I could barely make out, through one of the windows, the leaves of a tall, billowy tree moving ever so slightly in the thick warm air. Bzzzt. Bzzzt. The young man in front of me swatted at his bare arm. "Still the mind. Still the body," Myung-hee gently reminded us, seemingly unfazed by the mosquitoes flying in through the open windows and toward our warm-blooded human bodies. Bzzzt. Bzzzt. For the next hour, the group of us sat quietly meditating. We were barefoot seekers wearing baggy pants and short sleeves. But mostly, we were steak dinners.

Finally, the bell chimed, and the monk entered the meditation hall. He sat on a cushion, facing us. His eyes shining joyful and inquisitive. "I wonder," he began, "Where are you going?" Myung-hee sat beside him, translating Korean into English. *Where are you going?* Korean participants would travel, the following morning, to their hometowns for Chuseok to be with their families and honor their ancestors. "Chinhae," one of the participants said. "Kunsan," said another.

Where are you going? "Home," I answered.

The monk spoke in Korean -- gentle whirring sounds of "uhns" and "ees" -- nodding at each of us, pausing to breathe deeply and gaze out the windows at shadows in the moonlight. A mosquito landed on his forehead, above his left eyebrow. He didn't flinch. The Korean participants nodded slowly as the monk talked on – "hyeonjaeui sungan man-issda…" And on. When the monk clasped his hands and became silent, Myung-hee faced us three native English speakers. "No, you go different place," she interpreted. "More complicate."

Enroute back to my Seoul apartment, I stopped to go hiking at Buramsan Mountain range with its well-maintained trails that crisscrossed the Korean Peninsula like the head, heart, and lifelines of a farmer's palm. I hiked often in Korea, most weekends, enticed by the physical challenge and the majesty and grace of nature. Centering my backpack, I hiked at a quick, steady clip up footpaths, past Korean families picnicking with coolers and camper stoves. Upon reaching the rocky summit, I stood poised well-above the city streets and subway lines, box houses, and condominiums. Taking in the vast landscape, blinking my eyes at the wind, I had a sense of freedom. I felt far, far away, yet, strangely, as if I was inching my way home.

FERENGI

I heard the word while darting across dusty Addis Ababa streets or lingering in a grocery store aisle, price checking Corn Flakes. "Ferengi!" Ethiopia travel guidebooks will tell you that it's a term of endearment meaning *foreigner*. I'd traveled to Addis Ababa during our long winter break between Wangja University's fall and spring semesters. I was there to volunteer at an orphanage. Throughout the years, I'd found volunteering in various locales and capacities rewarding. I enjoyed communing with people from different places and cultures, settling into my service work routine. I even enjoyed staying in crappy five-dollar-a-night rooms. Feeling like I had a purpose. For the five weeks that I was in Addis Ababa, *ferengi* was sometimes used endearingly. Like the morning I sat in a café – four tables in a room with cracked, exposed drywall -- where rich, black coffee was served in tiny glasses with crystal handles as delicate as Cinderella's glass slipper. As I stirred raw sugar granules into my coffee, a gentleman with closely-shaved hair and perfect ears -- like toast-brown teapot handles – offered a wondrous smile. "Good morning, Ferengi."

Other times *ferengi* sounded clinical. I'd walk the pavement, past vendor shacks selling plastic bins and straw brooms. "Ferengi," a man in linen slacks or woman in head scarf or school-aged child in track pants would say. The way a person watching traffic from a park bench might note, "Volkswagen Beetle." At times a group of teenagers would spot me. Elbow one another. Yell out, "Hello! You! Hey, You! Ferengi!"

Occasionally, it seemed "Ferengi!" rose from a local's genuine excitement that some middle-aged woman from far, far away had sat on a cramped airplane for ten hours just to visit Ethiopia. Still, it got old. Being pointed at, yelled at, reminded that I was The Other.

In Addis Ababa, I found a room in a guest house. Not the kind of sunny kitchen guest house where a low-breasted woman named Gretel asks how you like your eggs cooked. The communal kitchen in my guest house had electrical wires hanging from its ceiling and a refrigerator that made a continual knocking sound as if a gerbil were trapped inside pounding the bottom shelf with its tiny, furred fists.

The kitchen was in a separate building, up a hill from the one-story string of six flimsy-walled guest rooms positioned side-by-side, reminding me of rooms at a no-tell motel. My single room contained a twin bed with dusty blanket and a ceiling-mounted lightbulb. Most of the other rooms were shared by two or three men. Siblings, perhaps. Or friends or co-workers.

We all shared a bathroom with two toilet stalls and one cold-water-only shower. Since both men and women shared the bathroom, the door could be unlocked from the outside with anyone's room key then dead-bolted from the inside. When I'd awaken with a full bladder at two o'clock in the morning, I'd have to step outside, lock my door, then run past three rooms in the dark to get to the dimly lit bathroom. Once inside the bathroom, I'd dead-bolt the door behind me, pee, then run back to my room, unlock my door and step inside feeling shivery with nerves from feeling disoriented and alone after dropping myself in an unfamiliar country where I didn't know the customs or speak the language, where I didn't know a soul.

I walked to the orphanage at 6:00 a.m. dressed in my volunteer uniform -- loose jeans, cotton T-shirt and old sneakers. It was a thirty-minute walk before sunrise and, unlike me, Addis Ababa was wide awake. I veered around strolling pedestrians carrying lunch sacks and briefcases. Around people piling in and out of twelve-seat vans, called micro-buses. Bald-tired buses revved at the curb, belching black exhaust. Smoker's cough.

The orphanage was situated on a narrow street beside vendor stalls selling bananas, avocado and thick-glass soda bottles of orange Fanta. It was in an area where pavement dwellers slept on newspapers, covered themselves with moth-eaten blankets. Small children in ragged pants and shoulder-torn T-shirts dashed about with soot-blackened feet. These children held out, to passersby, their flattened palms with grimed lifelines. Spotting me, one or two would rush over. "Ferengi!" they'd say, tilting up shiny faces, smiling with their baby-corn teeth. And I'd think, *You're so little to be over here by yourself. Where's your Mama?* I'd glance at a section of sidewalk where two mothers in soiled gypsy-skirts nursed babies and held cups out for spare change. I'd reach into my canvas bag and dole out bananas thinking, strangely, out of the blue, *That could be me.*

Orphanage babies were located upstairs from the well-swept, open bay area where pre-school-aged children slept on cots in neat rows. On a bookshelf lay a worn, one-eyed Teddy bear and rag doll. Enclosed porches housed Hoola-Hoops, dinged-aluminum wagons, and plastic bats with wiffle balls. From strung clothes lines hung pint-sized elastic-waist jeans, ruffle-hemmed nightgowns, cotton socks and T-shirts. Donated orphan issue.

I followed my nose up the wooden staircase to where the babies lived. The smell wasn't overpowering, but it presented itself in wafts. A combined odor of raw oats, sour milk, urine, and something primal, mushy, and possibly green. The baby floor included a spacious room with cribs and changing tables, stacks of washed clothes and crib sheets. There was an adjoining washroom where nursery workers wiped down drooly infants and hosed off poopy diapers. Across the hallway, in a small kitchen area, female Ethiopian staff workers stirred pots of oatmeal and sliced overripe bananas. Unsure of where to go, I lingered at the entrance of the playroom – a space where babies, ranging in age from four to eighteen months, were supervised and fed and given room to socialize and play. A handful of women cared for these orphans. More than twenty babies and children downstairs. They rocked sleepy infants and kissed chubby faces. Most of their time was devoted to navigating daily tasks in quick motion. Bottle feeding babies, trimming tiny fingernails, swabbing waxy ears, laundering blankets, cleaning toys, and shaving toddlers' heads to control the proliferation of lice.

I stepped inside the playroom and made eye contact with a childcare worker who sat on the floor. She was plump and cocoa skinned. Cradling one child in her arm and patting the back of another baby who lay draped across her lap, she waved at me and smiled. The outside corners of her large, dark eyes sloped downward, like a Kewpie doll, making her appear happy and sad all at once. While the Ethiopian workers spoke Amharic, some had memorized a few key English words that came in handy for directing international volunteers. *Wash. Cookie. Help.* She pointed to the bowls of oatmeal situated beside her. "Feed," she said. I sat on a blanket on the floor. Nine babies lay on their backs clenching plastic rattles, sucking on doughy fists, laying on their bellies and banging alphabet blocks against the floor. I brushed my finger along one baby's cheek. "Hello, sweetie." I cupped my hand atop another baby's peach-fuzzed scalp. "Hey, cutie." Babies. All cottony and warm and blubber-kneed. Some toothless, all gums. Others smiling with hamster teeth. All with heads so big and round like globes of the world.

Along the perimeter of the room, a few toddlers raced around, pushing the scuffed Fisher Price shopping cart or Little Tikes lawn mower. One of the toddlers shoved her plastic shopping cart into a toy truck. "Ayana!" the worker reprimanded. Ayana was about eighteen months old. She was solidly built. Had a sturdy trunk and thick, coffee-table legs. She tightened her grip on the handle, gained momentum, and rammed the cart into the wall. For someone in a diaper, she seemed awfully strong.

Ayana glanced over at the woman. Pushed her shopping cart into a pile of blocks. Rolled it over a stuffed bunny. Ayana had a skin condition that made her shaved head rashy and her face kind of pimply or waffly, like the crust of an Oreo cookie. The worker said something in Amharic, probably reminding the toddler to play nice.

I once held a newborn in India who'd been dragged along the sidewalk by her still-attached umbilical cord. Her mentally ill mother had given birth to her then walked the pavement unaware. The newborn was fine. She'd physically recovered from minor injuries within a day or two. She was the most beautiful baby I'd ever seen – fawn-eyed with a heart-shaped face and bumble-bee lips. She'd be adopted in an instant. A beautiful newborn with a sad, sensational story.

Ayana pushed her cart along the outskirts of the room, rolling it over wooden puzzle pieces and story books made of cloth. The worker gently rolled one baby off her lap and plopped the other baby on its diapered bottom facing me. Little Buddha. Then she left. Disappeared into the crib room to tend to newborns.

I was the lone adult in a room full of babies. Surrounded. Buddha baby went, "Eh, eh, uh!" I spooned oatmeal from the bowl and slid a pile between her gums. She flapped her arms, happy again. *Mission accomplished.* Another baby low-crawled toward me. "Eh! Eh!" I armed myself with a spoon of oatmeal, cupped her dimpled chin, scooped it into her open mouth.

A baby boy looked up at me, his bottom lip trembling and dark eyes filling with tears. He wore a blue bib embroidered, *Thank Heaven for Little Boys.* He flailed tiny fists like Rock 'em Sock 'em Robot. "Mmmmwwaaa!" "Wwaa!" In one hand, he gripped a toy. A small stuffed starfish in matted yellow fabric. It blurred as he punched the air. "Wwaaa!" Chain reaction. The other babies chimed, "Wwaaa!" Their lips stretched tight, nostrils flared, wisps of fine hair damp with sweat.

"It's okay. It's okay," I said. But it wasn't, of course. The babies wanted oatmeal, cookies, undivided attention, parents.

"Mmmwwaaa! Waaaaa!" baby boy screamed. His face was red, his mouth gaping like an open wound.

One of the nursery workers, carrying a stack of cloth diapers, walked past on her way to the crib room. "Bounce," she called over her shoulder. She nodded toward a swing suspended from the ceiling on bungy-cord-like cables.

I picked up baby boy, cradled my hands under his baby armpits. He kept a firm grip on the fuzzy starfish. "Let's go bounce." Stepping carefully around the others, I pulled baby boy's face against my chest. I carried him to the swing then pulled his fat little feet through the two holes of the padded bouncy seat. "Bouncy," I said in an unnaturally high voice. The swing hung just low enough for baby boy to plant his heels on the floor and push up, initiating a bouncing momentum. He waved his arms. Happy. "Yes, bouncy!" Then he dropped the starfish toy.

From the perimeter, Ayana spotted the yellow starfish. She abandoned her plastic shopping cart. Rushed over.

Two other babies noticed that the starfish was up-for-grabs and lumbered toward the toy like sea lions to a clam bucket. Ayana plowed through them, stomping on the baby's hand nearest the toy.

"Oh, no!" I said to Ayana. The other baby shrieked, its chest heaving then collapsing into sobs. "Not okay, Ayana." Kneeling, I patted the back of the crying baby then reached for the starfish -- a smiley face with cheerful-oval eyes sewn into its fabric. Ayana faced me with a sable, hardened glare and I backed away from the toy. She grasped the starfish with her chubby hand. Then thundered, her thickly diapered bottom twisting side to side, back to her cart to patrol the perimeter.

I walked miles along Addis Ababa sidewalks, looping the city center, zigzagging down narrow streets. A man nudged his friend. "Ferengi," he said. A lanky teenage boy, holding the hand of his little sister looked over. "Hey, you!" the teen yelled.

"You! Ferengi!" The little sister jumped up and down. Pointed my way. "Ferengi! Ferengi!"

One Saturday, I visited the National Museum of Ethiopia. Spent most of my time in the basement staring through glass at a skeletal cast of the fossilized hominid, *Lucy*, posed walking, her chin held high. I exited the museum, stepping into sunlight. A man and woman were approaching the entrance. They were silver haired. Wore eyeglasses and brimmed hats the color of pebble. They were dressed in peat moss cargo pants and lightweight, pocketed vests. Right off the pages of a clothing catalog for financially comfortable world travelers. The woman carried an Ethiopia guidebook in one hand. The man shouldered a small backpack. They held hands. They looked a team. I felt a warm flush of desire. They were explorers, together. Who needed a compass when they had one another? I named them the Travelsmiths.

Chills. Fever. Diarrhea. Nausea. The left side of my abdomen ached. Is the appendix on my left, or right? In my room, I had one large bottle of filtered water left. Two bananas. I felt thirsty. Earlier, on my way to the orphanage, I'd walked past a hospital building. Its roof tiles were peeling, its windows duct taped. A line of infirmed waited in the parking lot outside the emergency department. I didn't speak Amharic. Didn't know how to navigate the medical system here. I pressed a hand to the nape of my neck. My skin felt on fire. I felt all alone.

I fell into a restless sleep and woke up parched two hours later and drank half my water. When I fell back asleep, I dreamt about the Travelsmiths. They were walking past a hospital in utter disrepair, nodding at the infirmed, some of whom were standing, others who sat on a concrete sidewalk or lay on their sides on threadbare blankets. Mrs. Travelsmith carried her guidebook. Mr. Travelsmith shouldered his backpack. They were still holding hands.

There's a town in northern Ethiopia named Lalibella where, during the 12th century, eleven medieval monolithic churches were hewn from red rock. I'd flown to Lalibella through turbulent skies. The prop plane flew through dark clouds. Quick tilts left and right. Queasy stomach ups and downs. Adult passengers clutched their armrests, pressed their heads against backrests. We were silent. On a journey through hell. A little girl, about four years old, giggled. Then laughed. Wee! she said. She was on a roller coaster ride. I supposed it was all a matter of perspective. The plane remained steadily airborne then safely landed.

Rather than being built from the ground up, the medieval Lalibella churches had been carved from the earth. Monolithic blocks had been chiseled -- creating walls, doors, windows, floors, columns. When visionaries first approached this landscape with a desire to construct places of worship, I imagine the challenges of such an undertaking seemed nearly insurmountable. Yet, once they broke through the surface, they must have realized its potential and proceeded to sculpt the churches from rock, uncovering the beauty that had been there all along.

On a patch of asphalt and dirt outside the orphanage, children jumped rope and dribbled balls and played on a rusted metal swing set. One morning, I neared the building and saw a child pushing a toddler on a swing. "Wee!" the child said, pushing the swing higher and higher. The toddler stiffened with fear, her small fists clenching the swing's chain. "Wee!" The child pushed. I quickened my pace toward the playground, motioning for the child to slow the swing. The toddler held tight to the chains and lowered her feet toward the ground. The swing was still airborne. When the swing descended, the toddler dropped her feet against the dusty asphalt. Put the brakes on her momentum. The swing slowed but didn't stop. The toddler's legs were once again airborne. Upon the next descent, her feet hit the ground hard. She released her grip. Plopped to the ground on her diapered bottom and fell backwards. Fortunately. The empty wooden seat swung over her body.

I ran to her. Caught the swing. The toddler scrambled to her feet. "Ayana!" I'd hardly recognized her apart from the baby room. Playing outdoors on her own like a big girl. "Hey, Baby Girl!" I squatted down, extended my arms. She rushed into me, arms reaching, placed her hands on the sides of my waist, gesturing for a hug. She stood rigid with a tense-shouldered hesitance then said, "Up!" I wrapped one arm around Ayana's sturdy frame, propped the other beneath her bottom then stood, balancing her on my hip.

I caught Ayana's gaze – syrupy and quizzical – and gave a bouncing skip. Ayana let out a choppy laugh. "Bouncy!" I said. Ayana tilted up her face, flashed her baby-corn teeth. She leaned into me, for a moment, unwary. I pulled her snug. Wished I could take her with me. Welcome her into a loving home where we'd be a team, she and I. Where she'd no longer seem The Other, pushing a cart along the perimeter. As if it were that easy. Sign some papers. Save a baby. Ayana breathed out, relaxed and still, and I kissed the creases of her warm neck the rich color of loam, the smell of salty earth, the center of the earth.

Bottoms Up

Usuhan, a top-tier university in Korea, posted an employment ad for an English professor. I met their qualifications and licked my lips at the prospect of being hired at Usuhan. For the past year, I'd worked as an instructor at Wangja University. At Usuhan, I'd be a *professor.* I'd earn more money, enrich my curriculum vitae and imagined feeling suddenly erudite and dapper in tweed. There was one catch. The vacant position was at Usuhan's Daehag campus. If hired, I'd have to move from Seoul, with its vibrant metropolis of twenty-five million, to Daehag, a tired city of 300,000. Living in Daehag would intensify my language barrier. I'd have limited access to English-subtitled restaurant menus. Or doctors, dentists, bank clerks with comprehensible English.

I took the ninety-minute train ride from Seoul to Daehag. Then a taxi to campus past a ten-kilometer stretch of rice paddies, cabbage fields and isolated clusters of apartment buildings with 7-Elevens and chicken eateries. I arrived early for my interview, marked time by strolling campus sidewalks. It was spring. Blooming pale-yellow forsythia and lavender rhododendron accented paths and entryways, lined the fronts of academic buildings, breaking up brick façade. The interview was held in the four-story Campus Building A12 -- the same building where English classes were conducted. The corridors of A12 were lined with boxes of printer paper and smudged desks pushed against walls. It was Saturday morning. No students roamed the hallways. A custodian – squat and dour-faced – rolled his mop bucket in a lazy S.

The trash cans in the ladies' room were heaped with soiled tissues. Black strands of hair lay in the sink. Wadded bags of potato chips littered the countertop. I stood in front of the mirror, rehearsing answers to commonly asked interview questions. What is your greatest professional strength? *My teaching evaluations have consistently shown that students find me well-prepared, organized and committed to engaging in innovative teaching practices to bolster learning.* What do you consider to be your weakness? *I used to hesitate to speak up at staff meetings. I've learned to feel more comfortable with cooperative decision-making and wholehearted participation.* Interview bullshit. I wanted to wow them. To win. In spite of the heightened language barrier I'd face in Daehag, along with the anticipated boredom I might experience living in a rural environ, I convinced myself that job promotion victory would offset these challenges. Besides, the initial thrill of living in Seoul had begun to dissipate. The restlessness I'd experienced in the U.S. had somehow caught up with me halfway around the world. In my mind, I created a vision worth moving toward -- a new life in Daehag in which I'd roam country lanes, exchange pleasantries with farmers selling homegrown potatoes, corn, and radishes. There was something so hopeful about leaving one place and going to another.

"Laurie Woodford?" the Assistant Dean, a Korean woman in her fifties, extended her hand, bowing slightly. "I'm Dr. Park." She wore a pressed navy skirt and white shirt with starched collar. Her black pumps appeared spit-shined. "Please meet Trevor," she said, gesturing toward a stout, warm-eyed man. "And Charlie," she added.

"Pleased to meet you." Charlie gave a quick shake of my hand. Trevor and Charlie were professors at Usuhan, so they were my potential colleagues. They were from New Zealand. A place I imagined good natured chaps throwing around words like *arsehole* and *wanker.* Giving their friends fun-hearted slaps on the back while telling them to *Piss off, mate.*

Trevor asked most of the questions. What textbooks had I used at Wangja University? What challenges had I faced in the classroom? How had I created rapport with my students? A polite round of questions and gentle follow-ups. *I like them.*

Charlie piped in every now and then. "Can you tell us about your professional strengths...Weaknesses?" My rehearsed answers sounded thoughtful, natural even. Glancing at my curriculum vitae, Charlie said, "Nice. I see you taught English Composition in New York. And you've worked with students from beginner level to advanced…" He and Dr. Park twisted their necks, eyeing me then one another as if moonstruck. *Ooh, I think they like me too.*

I saw a bright future. Me and my wankers chatting after class. Going out for a pint. Answering questions with a congenial, "Yeah-nah, not really, eh, mate."

They wanted me. I'd won.

Most of the English classes I taught at Usuhan were held on campus. On Friday mornings, however, I taught a three-hour English listening/speaking class to Usuhan medical students at Daehag Christian Hospital. At seven o'clock, I gathered my briefcase and walked a few blocks to catch my bus.

In South Korea, public drunkenness didn't seem frowned upon. As I walked to the bus stop, the sidewalk bore the aftereffects of Thursday night partying. Cherry-pie-sized splatters of dried vomit. As if balloons filled with spaghetti sauce mixed with chunky peanut butter had been dropped from a third-floor window. Splat! I waited for clunky Bus 404 which would weave me through Daehag city streets for thirty-five minutes before dumping me at the hospital.

Our class was held in a white-walled conference room, its tall windows facing a row of parked ambulances. At night, medical students congregated in that room to study for their next exam. Identify the Median Cubital. Brachioradialis. The Calcaneus. I arrived early and opened the door to a blast of stale air. The smell of old asparagus and garlic paste.

"Good morning! Happy Friday!" I said. The medical students raised their heads groggily. Strands of black hair stuck to their cheeks. They slept head-planted on the table surface amidst stacked medical books and candy wrappers, so apple-red sleep marks were pressed into their foreheads. Yawning, they sifted through crumpled notes then exited the room. My students filed in. There were sixteen total. Mostly young men who sat bleary-eyed and hung over.

"Good morning, Laurie teacher," they said. Spoken in croaks. Thursday night was Upperclassmen night. My male students – Lowerclassmen -- could not refuse a drink from higher-ranking peers. They binge drank until the wee hours of Friday morning and, now, here they were facing a three-hour English class.

"Ten minutes 'til showtime," I announced. Last week, I'd assigned small group presentations. In groups of four they were to present on the history, architecture, cultural attractions, and personality of a city of their choice. Each group member had a mandatory speaking part. I graded on organization of information, public speaking skills and individual English proficiency. I'd promised them ten minutes at the beginning of class to rehearse before presenting.

"Need more time please," Mu-yeol said, forcing a smile. "Maybe fifteen minute, Laurie teacher?" Mu-yeol was tall, lean, and square-jawed with large, cedar-brown eyes. He was handsome when he wasn't hungover. No doubt, last night, he'd consumed too much soju -- a cheap, tasteless 20 proof alcohol that sold for under two dollars per ten-ounce bottle. Soju could be purchased at grocers and convenience stores in bottles up to 72 ounces. Many Koreans drank soju while hiking, on picnics, with dinner. They drank soju while sitting on plastic chairs outside 7-Elevens until the sun rose and the subway and buses began running. Then they'd stumble their way to the station.

It was difficult to look at Mu-yeol. The capillaries in his eyes had burst, forming tiny red spider stars. His face was swollen and blotchy. His eyes bulged, as if he hung in a noose. *Jesus. At least I don't get that bad.* In Korea, I'd started drinking more. At first, I attributed my increased alcohol consumption – the incremental, but steadfast, climb in the number of bottles of beer or glasses of wine I drank each night after work -- to cultural norm and ease of accessibility. The neon-lit signs above convenience stores located at nearly every corner blinked 24/7, summoning passersby to purchase wine, beer, hard liquor. I'd stock up. Slide 32-ounce beer cans and bottles of soju onto the check-out counter without a tinge of self-consciousness. In the U.S., I might have pictured a judgmental glance from the patron standing behind me in line, or the store clerk bagging my items. What a curious purchase, I might have imagined them thinking. A middle-aged woman buying beer and hard liquor on a Monday evening. As my time in Korea went on, I grew curious myself. Was I drinking more to soothe my feelings of isolation? To numb the emotional fallout from saying goodbye to so many, from leaving so much behind?

My apartment here in Daehag was dingy, with little natural light filtering through panes of frosted glass. I sometimes splashed soju into my beer glass while sitting cross-legged on the bed, staring at my apartment's walls which were yellowed and layered with tar and nicotine build-up from former chain-smoking tenants. When I first arrived, I'd scrubbed the walls with rags saturated in vinegar, ammonia, lemon juice. Application after application, but still an impenetrable film remained. Rag water dripped a sick brownish yellow, the color of sulphur water trickling from a rusted pipe.

During the day, sober, my dismal surroundings could send me into a funk. Leave me pining for my tidy and bright ranch house in Rochester that I'd rented out. *How did I end up here? I used to live in a pretty house.* I hadn't taken my Rochester domicile for granted when I lived there. I'd appreciated its aesthetics. My fireplace mantel decorated with candles and ceramic vases. My living room sofa cozied up with turquoise throw pillows. My quiet patio surrounded with hydrangea and peonies. The day I'd rented out that house to a young family with two kids and a parakeet, I'd felt a tug at my heart. Yet, somehow, I hadn't expected to miss it. I was moving on, turning a new page in my life, I'd decided. A life untethered, free from the weight of material possessions.

Here, in Korea, I made a conscious effort to avoid acquiring stuff. I grooved into minimalism, limiting decorations in my apartment to a handful of printed 4x6-inch photos of family and friends taped to the door of my rickety wardrobe. I was pleased with my discipline, my ability to keep attachment to things at bay. But every now and then, I longed to come home to a space that extended the invitation: Welcome, make yourself comfortable. Make yourself at home.

When drunk on soju or wine, my funk over the bleak space in which I lived lifted, like a ring of cigarette smoke floating toward light, stretching indistinct, then breaking apart, losing grip. And I turned more quizzical than despairing. *If the inside of this yellowed, stained apartment looks this bad, what must the insides of the former tenants' chain-smoking lungs look like?*

I stood at the table where Mu-yeol's group congregated. "Okay," I said. "You may have fifteen minutes to rehearse."

"Thank you, Laurie teacher," Mu-yeol said. "Now you are my best friend." Mu-yeol's classmates involuntarily blinked, jerked back an inch as he spoke. Soju breath.

As students rehearsed their presentations, I flipped through a textbook thinking about the upcoming weekend. It was Friday night, and I had no social plans. I'd walk the hilly, five-kilometer-long dirt road that circled behind campus. The *fire walk*, my colleagues called it. The road provided a forest fire barrier between the mountain's densely treed upper tier and university buildings. I walked the loop daily. Oftentimes twice. Sometimes a third time, circling round the fire walk, like a walkabout. Always alone.

After fifteen minutes passed, I pointed to the wall-clock. "It's time."

My first group of presenters dimmed the classroom's overhead lights, turned on the projector and clicked their PowerPoint on slideshow. Mu-yeol spoke enthusiastically. "We like introduce to you Paris. City of romance!"

*

My colleagues and I lived rent-free in a twelve-building apartment complex near campus. A pine forest bordered north and east ends of the property. I was told the complex's translated name was something like Tree Look. There were twenty of us foreigners living in the complex. Most residents in Tree Look were Korean. That made foreign faculty easy to spot when making the fifteen-minute walk to class or ducking into the apartment complex's convenience store. We stood out with our rough-featured faces, big feet and all.

Walking home one Friday afternoon after class, I noticed my colleagues, Tricia and Max, strolling about ten yards ahead. They were Americans who taught Intermediate Reading and Advanced Writing to Usuhan college freshmen.

They were in love. I knew this from the way Tricia rubbed her hand along the back of Max's neck. The way Max paused to touch his forehead to hers. Tricia confided that, last Saturday, she and Max stayed in bed all day watching *Game of Thrones*. Between episodes he'd made her orgasm six times. Six times! she repeated.

I slowed my pace. Leave room for the lovers. Eventually Tricia and Max noticed me lurking behind. "Laurie!" they called. "We're stopping at Gasijo for a beer or two. Come with us!"

"Oh, thanks, but…"

"Come on, it's Friday!"

At Gasijo, Tricia and I claimed a table while Max ordered drinks at the bar and, eventually, returned gripping three mugs of Hite Stout. Tricia gazed up at him through blonde bangs. "Thank you, Hon," she said. "It's the weekend, finally!" she added. "Laurie, do you have any plans?"

"I'll probably hike Chiaksan," I told them. "Either tomorrow or Sunday." As Tricia and I sipped beer, Max pushed his chair back, an arm's length from the table, planted his palms on the seat of his chair and stretched his legs out. Crossing his left ankle over right, he lifted his hips into an isometric hold. Max was a gym rat who worked out every moment he could. After ten seconds or so, he relaxed his body back into the chair.

"Hiking. That sounds neat," Tricia said, tracing a finger along Max's shoulder then over his bulging bicep.

"Yeah, cool," Max added. Crossing his right ankle over left, he lifted his buttocks into an isometric hold again, forming a straight plank from ankles to shoulders.

"Max and I are taking a day-trip to Seoul," Tricia said. They'd take an early train into the city and a late train home. *That might put a dent in her six orgasms. She may only get four.*

"I want to shop for a Samsung tablet," Max said, tucking his chin in to check out his taut body held in a plank. Then he began contracting muscles, rhythmically tightening his hamstrings and glutes. *Jesus, what's he doing? Ass enhancers?*

"We're also buying a toaster oven," Tricia added, then lifted her chin toward Max. "We're going to move in together."

"That's wonderful," I said, smiling at Tricia then Max. I sipped my beer. *I wish he'd stop flexing his ass.*

It surprised me to learn that many Korean women slept with stuffed animals. My student, Ha-yoon, pointed to a photo of her shared dorm room. Its bunk bed mattresses were piled with Teddy bears and plushy, pink puppies. Was that typical? I asked her. "Yes. Very," Ha-yoon said. After that, I noticed them everywhere. On the subway button-eyed sock monkeys peeked from open purses. In the park fuzzy yellow hedgehogs sat on benches beside their adult owners. Culture of cuteness. *Kawaii* in Japan had caught on in South Korea. One afternoon I walked past a neighborhood bar. Two Korean twenty-somethings sat drinking beer. One held a floppy, blue bunny in her lap. The other a purple unicorn with wings. I shook my head. *Aren't you embarrassed?*

A month later I saw a woman with a giant, stuffed Panda in her bicycle basket. I kicked a pebble down the sidewalk. *It must feel nice to hold something close at night.*

My online dating inbox had been bone-dry for months. One night I indulged a fantasy. Thought about dates I'd had in Rochester. Wondered what Match.com Jim with the wandering eye was doing these days. Perhaps I'd jumped to the wrong conclusion about him, and he'd rambled on about his dating disappointments from pure nervousness. Perhaps back in Rochester, where it seemed I had dating options, I was too hasty throwing in the towel when a man I met for coffee didn't immediately feel like a match.

Opening my laptop, I told myself, "Just give it time. As Jeung-hun said, 'There are many bright fish in the ocean.'" Then I noticed a lengthy BeMineInternation.com message from a thirty-eight-year-old man from India.

Hello! Beautiful n charming lady! the message began. *I am a very simple and ordinary Man. Kind hearted, fun to be with, very sincere. Friendly, honest and loving person. I am non-smoker and dislike alcohol.* Next he went in for the big sell. *Like every person, I have advantages and disadvantages. I'm a disabled guy, earn nothing and am not well educated. I can't stand up on my legs. My whole body is very weak n thin. I fall down easily. Even I just know little bit of English n I'm just 5th grade pass. I don't know how to* *multiply n divide. Let's know each other better! Please reply soon, Beautiful Lady!*

I closed my laptop. Were these my choices now that I was a menopausal expat living in Asia? Either fantasizing about past dates gone badly or corresponding with an unemployed, brittle-boned man who didn't know that two times two equals four? I rubbed the back of my neck, studying my yellowed walls.

The following afternoon, in the hallway of Campus Building A12, I lingered a few paces behind Tricia and Max. We were on our way to classroom 306 for our departmental staff meeting where nineteen of us English teachers would sit in hard chairs drinking cans of bubble tea and discussing student assessment. During that meeting, while Trevor talked about Written Corrective Feedback and customized grading rubrics, I noticed that my American colleague, Steve, had a great head of hair. Steve was a thirty-nine-year-old music hipster of sorts. He routinely wore clunky, ear-muff-type headphones around his neck, like an air travel pillow. His hair was horse-brown and full. It bounced when he shuffled down campus sidewalks, on the balls of his feet, weighted forward, like a giant toddler. "Hey, Laurie." Steve approached me in the hallway one afternoon after class. "Could you send me that grammar handout you talked about in the meeting?"

"Sure, I'd be happy to," I told him. Then we got talking about some independent film we both liked and my body began to feel light, like a Retriever chasing a ball. *He's kind of cool.* We got laughing about a lesson in our English textbook that featured an Argentine gaucho and Steve's eyes flashed starry as he laughed. *Does he think I'm kind of cool, too?*

That Saturday night, I agreed to join nine colleagues, including Steve, for drinks and dinner. I spent extra time getting ready for the evening, brushing on matte eye shadow, smoothing product in my hair. We all met at the Grove – a local wood-paneled restaurant that dished up chicken and kimchi and microwaveable Hawaiian pizza. A cross-culture tiki bar. Our Usuhan crew – Americans and New Zealanders -- started with drinks, jovially slapping Korean Won on the bar counter. We occupied the outdoor patio, ordered pizza and wings, meandered from table to table, mingling, laughing. "Another round of vodka tonics and beer!" we cheered.

Just a week earlier, I'd taken my foster dog to her new home. I hadn't planned to foster a pet. I'd volunteered at an animal shelter, walking dogs one weekend, and made an emotional connection with a fifteen-pound mutt described as a Terrier mix. She was wire-haired, short-legged, tense in the shoulders. I'd seen a Google image of a Portuguese Podengo Pequeno and decided that's what she was and named her Podengo. Podengo had lived at the shelter for years, escaping a few times and returned by animal control. At the end of the day at the shelter, I took Podengo for a second walk. I clipped the retractable leash to her collar and followed her down a dirt road near the facility. Halfway through our walk, she halted, tucked her chin, wriggled out of her collar, and took off in a flash. I chased after, but she was far ahead. "Here, girl!" I yelled. "Come on, girl!" Upon hearing my voice, Podengo stopped then turned. Her blonde fur bounced in waves as she ran to me.

Her response to my voice, her willingness to abandon momentary freedom and turn toward me was a sign, I decided. A kinship had been actualized; we were meant to be together.

Two weeks later, after my foster application was approved, I arrived at the shelter to pick up the dog. She looked groggy. I walked her to the bus stop. We took the bus to the subway, then the subway to a taxi. Once in my apartment, I fed her a scoop of canned dog food from my cupped palm. She took a few bites, looked up at me with moist eyes. I removed what looked like a wide, ace bandage that had been wrapped around her lower waist and rump. I foolishly thought the animal shelter staff had put a diaper on her for our long trek home on public transportation. When I removed the cloth wrap, I noticed that fur had been shaved from her underbelly. I patted the floor, motioning for her to lie down then gently rolled her onto her back and studied the butterfly bandages placed over a jagged incision, her flesh held together with surgical glue. She'd recently been spayed. Reproductively, like me, she'd reached the end of an era.

Later, I carefully bathed her. Clipped her toenails. Swabbed her ears with Q-tips. Brushed her fur from nape to tail with a slicker. That night, she slept on my twin bed with her head just below my pillow. I draped my arm across her chest and fell asleep to the sound of her breathing. It felt nice to hold something close at night.

A few months later at my university, a note was distributed to foreign faculty. Reminder: NO PETS ALLOWED. At our apartment complex, many Korean tenants walked their dogs, carried bags of cat food from the store to their apartments. I'd surmised it was a pet-friendly environment. But now this. Horrified by the thought of returning Podengo to the shelter, I decided to lay low. Each morning and evening, before taking Podengo out to walk a wooded trail behind my apartment building, I cracked open my door, stuck my head out, looked both ways -- Coast clear? – then led her briskly to the trail.

Then one afternoon, while walking Podengo, I crossed paths with a colleague who shuffled slowly beside his toddler. "Oh, you have a dog," he said, then glanced down at his son. "Look, a doggy!" The child toddled toward Podengo, who'd always been a friendly dog with me and other volunteers. Apparently, Podengo disliked toddlers. She bared her teeth and growled and that Monday morning at work, another notice was distributed. Second Reminder: NO PETS ALLOWED.

I'd managed to keep Podengo for four months and was heartbroken at the prospect of having to give her up. I made it my mission to find her another foster person. On a website for expats living in South Korea, I read a thread of posts by people interested in adopting a pet. I learned about an American woman, an English teacher settling long-term in Korea, who wanted a small dog. I contacted her, sent photos of Podengo, and explained the situation at my apartment complex. She responded immediately, asked to meet Podengo and the dog and woman fell in love instantly. We contacted the shelter and transferred guardianship. A few days later, the woman sent me a video of Podengo wagging her tail then dancing on two legs for a Pup-Peroni. I'd found my foster dog a loving home. I cried for days.

Now, at the Grove, clinking liquor glasses with colleagues, I enjoyed a respite from my grief. Our Usuhan party group migrated to a beer joint with wooden benches and fluorescent lighting. It was located in the grid of restaurants a ten-minute walk from our apartment complex. By midnight, our group of ten had waned to seven. My stomach had turned alcohol-warm, the inside of my throat finely sand-papered from laughter. I studied Steve's tousled hair, his artsy eyeglasses. My beer mug was half full.

Trevor thumped an empty pitcher on the table. "Are we keen to go off to another bar, mates?" It was past two o'clock in the morning and our group was down to four -- me, Steve, Trevor and his wife, Julie. "Yeah, nah," Julie said, raising her nearly empty glass, "Churs!"

"Churs, mates!" I said. "Count me in!" Feeling free as a braless teenager.

At the next bar, Steve bought shots of whiskey and brought them to our table like communion glasses on an offering tray. To drink them we tossed our heads back hard. Under the table, Steve slid his hand onto mine. My long, dark hair flapped against his shoulder like a sail in the breeze. Steve's hand skated along the inseam of my jeans. He faced me with brown, liquid eyes. "Would you like to go home?" he asked, meaning to one of our apartments. *Hmmm.* I hesitated for a moment. *We're awfully drunk...* Steve said, "I'm not so drunk that I can't make a sound decision." I blinked slowly. Smiled. Then Steve was up paying the bill. And we were staggering home in the black night, stopping to pull our bodies together. My arms draped around Steve's neck, his hands cupped at the small of my back. Our mouths open, tongues sparring. Faint "ummms" of vulnerability fleeing into obsidian sky.

Soon we were unclad in my bed. Palms on bare shoulders, fingers palpating the spine, hands on bare asses. Backs hunching-arching, like yoga's cat and cow. Nothing new, really. We hadn't invented the thing. But that night, we were transported from our lackluster routines -- answering emails, grading papers, walking home alone from work -- and into wakefulness, surprise. Like a flashflood at springtime.

Then it was morning.

In daylight, the first thing my eyes focused on was Steve's exposed body which was planted face down in my bed. His toenails were unclipped, yellowed and ragged. *Jesus, he could saw through a French baguette with those things.* I felt vaguely panicked. And here I was in South Korea. The Land of the Morning Calm.

Of course, those toenails had been there all along. While we'd flirted in the hallway outside our classrooms, they lay in waiting underneath the leather tips of his work shoes. My age spots and sagging flesh had been there, too. Lurking beneath shirt sleeves, pressed beneath my camisole. Hidden and waiting for the big reveal. The kicking off of shoes. The rolling off of socks. The unbuttoning of a blouse. The undrawing of curtains that had kept unflattering illumination at bay.

A friend of mine once told me that, when she first met her partner, she admired his habit of walking around barefoot. "He walked around the house with no shoes, no socks. Not even flip-flops," she said wistfully. In her mind, it said something important about who he was. Free-spirited. Relaxed. All-natural. Not at all like her buttoned-up ex-husband. After living together for a year, dealing with family issues, reality set in. "I realized he walks around barefoot because his feet are hot." She sighed. "His feet are just hot all of the time."

Finding a partner at midlife differs from the ease of young love with its built-in possibilities. First home, first child, career promotion. Then bigger home, next child. Brand new minivan. Creating a life together from scratch offers the opportunity to grow and bond through shared children, common goals. With older love, the best you can hope for was that you both wanted a dog. A together dog. After the old ones from your former marriages, your former lives, had dropped dead from doggie cancer or heartworm.

That Monday morning, Steve and I met for coffee in a café on campus. It was awkward at first. We chatted through stiff smiles about work, plans for the weekend. Eventually we relaxed into relating to one another again through sober eyes. Perhaps we could go out for dinner on Friday night, Steve mentioned. Listen to music at his apartment, watch a movie at mine. *Might be fun.* I appreciated the flirtation. Enjoyed the zing. But I knew he and I were not relationship material. Maybe it was the age difference, our varied tastes in music and food, our disparate life trajectories. Or my knowing that our connection was merely a physical one that did not include the heart. We were not a match.

I'd slept with Steve because I'd gotten swept up in the moment. I was lonely. Drunk. Longing for touch, to feel desired. Most of all, I really missed my dog. Missed a loving, playful companion, a warm belly to scratch, the sound of contented sighs at night.

It seems things are rarely as we expect them to be. We open the pizza box to find anchovies instead of pepperoni. Try on a pair of skinny jeans only to look fat. We go to a party we're convinced will be a bore and end up having a great time.

It seemed to me that life was fluid. Changeable. Moment-to-moment flux inevitable. Perhaps, it was time for me to move on from Korea. Time to leave one place and go to another. Perhaps I could teach in another country, learn about a different culture. Or travel on a shoestring. Backpack. Explore. Volunteer. Meet people. Understand that life might turn, in an instant, from upside down to bottom side up.

Part II

Wading Into the Tide

Flash floods, the meteorologist warned. I was eight years old, standing in the kitchen eating dry Cocoa Puffs by the handful while my older brother studied for a math test upstairs. Our house, a Cape Cod with second-story window dormers protruded and peaked like surprised eyes, hummed a no-adults-home stillness that day after school. I stared out, through open curtains, at our backyard, a running stretch of closely mowed lawn. Outside, the rain poured. In the way-back part of our yard, the creek swelled. I ran out, past the rusted aluminum walls of our above ground pool, past the wire clothesline. I reached into my rabbit's coop, formed my small hand in a fist around Freddie's scruff. Cradling him to my chest, I tucked an arm beneath his belly, carried him from harm's way.

Indoors, sitting on my bed, I smoothed the damp, gray fur between Freddie's ears, his nose twitching with each shallow breath. The creek continued its heavy breathing -- exhale, hold, exhale, hold – rising into a sweep of muddied water, a rolling tide.

The babies! A few weeks earlier, my mother had brought home cardboard flats from DJ's Gardens of baby tomato, bell pepper, and cucumber plants. We'd planted the seedlings in full sun. Again, I bolted outside, barefoot, electric with adrenaline, running on soggy backyard grass into shin-deep then knee-deep water toward the tilled plot. Reaching underwater, into muck, I felt for life and pulled. Schluurrpp! Water surged, filling in where young roots had clung. Piling the plants into my T-shirt sling, I delivered them to raised patio brick then ran back again. My hands felt for supple limbs, which I grasped and yanked out.

Later, my mother stared, confused, at the heap of muddied stalks and leaves, at the pale roots reaching for solid ground. I told her I'd saved the babies from drowning. She laughed.

*

Now, wading ankle-deep in the Peruvian sea, past children patting sandy mud into castles, digging holes with tiny, brown hands, I hear that schlurping sound of water rushing in to fill the void.

I'd left Korea three months earlier then headed to South America, beginning in Ecuador then working my way to northern Peru. At the age of fifty-one, I was backpacking. A menopausal gap year.

Before embarking on my year of transience, I'd mulled over teaching options in other countries. There were jobs available in the Middle East, for example. A recruiter from Saudi Arabia requested an interview. But I had trepidations when I learned my passport would be kept by the school for two months while the Iqama – residence card – was being processed. I considered Spain or Italy, but the jobs were scarce for non-EU passport holders. I contemplated applying for jobs back home in the U.S., but good teaching positions seemed scarce in

Rochester, too. Besides, my house was being rented by a family of four. I needed to keep going, continue exploring. Time was irretrievable.

I'd decided to volunteer in Niebla, a small town of about 14,000 residents, some 300 kilometers from the Ecuador border. I'd stay five weeks at an animal rescue center located a few blocks from the beach. Despite this shoreline's can-see-forever ocean boundlessness, its white planked fishing boats bobbing on rippling waves, the waterfront felt devitalized. The air was thick with the smell of washed ashore bloated fish. The sky heavy and overcast in what appeared to me, a prehistoric, lifeless brown.

The day before, I'd stepped off a Huanchaco passenger bus onto packed dirt. A layer of silt dusted every surface – car bumpers, rooftops, the stooped shoulders of elderly women navigating broken sidewalks. This was northern Peru. A desert. No stately Machu-Pichuesque mountain ridges and ruins. No blue lagoon oasis. No llamas in straw hats. Only stretches of grey-beige sand and discarded plastic grocery bags, flattened like silhouettes against fences and prickly shrubs, wherever the wind had tossed and dead ended them.

The bus had been filled to capacity. I lingered outside with other passengers waiting to retrieve baggage stored in the bus's underbelly. The bus driver opened the steel door of the luggage hold. Wedged between a scuffed black suitcase and my red canvas backpack sat a tight-muscled man who sprang from the compartment. He delivered to the bus driver a thin seat cushion and cheerful, "Gracias, Senor." In Peru, it seemed, there was always room for one more.

The animal rescue center was owned by Wendy, an Australia native, who was leaving Peru to stay in Sydney for five weeks to visit her grown children. I'd learned about Wendy from a work exchange website where farmers or hostel owners or harried parents in need of free help posted profiles offering decent housing, three meals a day and a desire to treat the right volunteer just like family. In turn, backpackers like myself craving free room and board posted bios promising a solid work ethic, positive attitude and unwavering commitment to personal hygiene. That website was the Match.com of volunteerism. Wendy needed a reliable individual to house sit and oversee her animal rescue center. Most backpackers profiled on the website were fresh faced twenty-somethings. Wendy read my bio and initiated an email courtship. She was all hot for my "maturity."

"Niebla?" I asked the bus driver. He gestured to a man seated in a dusty station wagon parked and idling, waiting for passengers. I squeezed into the back seat, pressed hip-to-hip with a woman in denim stretch pants. Our colectivo rolled past flat desert bordered by mountain ridges that appeared makeshift, unstable, as if a God-sized dump truck had unloaded mounds of sand.

The driver parked the colectivo on a narrow street near the beach. "Senorita Wendy?" I asked.

"Wendy? Animales?" He pointed north.

A sign with painted silhouettes of a cat and dog was posted in front of Wendy's place. Her property was enclosed by a wooden planked privacy fence. A wreath of dried lilies and camu camu berries hung on the front gate. I raised a hand to knock. Wendy opened the door. A solidly built woman in her sixties, Wendy pulled me into her bosom. "Thank Heavens," she said. She was SO happy to see me. So relieved that I'd shown up! In the past, she'd been burned by irresponsible volunteers. Baby-faced assholes. She never really doubted ME, of course. A mature woman like herself. She was just so glad to see me. We'd celebrate, she and I. She'd roast a chicken. A chicken she'd paid SIX DOLLARS for. Six dollars for CHICKEN. Highway robbery. "That's Peru for ya," she added.

The rescue center was really Wendy's home, set on an acre of land, which had evolved into an animal sanctuary, step by step, year by year, stray by stray. More than a decade earlier, Wendy had taken in a few starved dogs, their furred ribs showing through like xylophone keys. Shortly after, she bottle-fed an abandoned litter of mite-infested kittens. When a neighbor brought over a box of puppies with worm-bloated bellies, she welcomed them. There was always room for one more.

Her property was now a refuge for four-legged misfortunates, a Francis of Assisi-type gated community for the infirmed. Wendy's home was a conglomeration of free-standing structures – neither sheds nor cabins, exactly, something in between. That was typical in the warm, arid climate of northern Peru. Why confine oneself indoors, living in one blocky building comprised of rooms separated by drywall, when one could move freely from room to room, through fresh air instead?

Wendy's home consisted of four cottages situated in half moon, facing a garden of closely packed potted Hibiscus and an expanse of sparse, dry lawn dotted with wire clotheslines. Cottage One was the bedroom and bath where Wendy slept. Beside that stood the kitchen cottage with attached porch sheltering a heavy, mosaic-finished dining table. A couple of guest cottages with bedrooms and baths completed the composite, each with aluminum shingled roofs on which hard-eyed cats sunned by day and scrambled over come nightfall.

The center included capacious kennels with domed dog houses and KONG goodie bones, as if the canines had won a game show spin and been awarded deluxe accommodations. The fifty or so cats lived in uncrowded coops with multi-tiered kitty playgrounds and quilted baskets. In a brick-walled enclosure, two tortoises with sad histories pulled their shelled bulk with thick, wrinkled clawed feet.

A fifth cottage near Wendy's gravel driveway had been added – a pint-sized veterinary clinic -- which housed an examination table and glass-doored cabinet stocked with packets of gauze, rubbing alcohol, syringes. Stacked in the clinic's corners were empty dog crates and hard-plastic bins crammed with donated baby blankets and towels.

While the occasional hound with a fractured leg or feline with belly tumors were carted into the rescue center's veterinary clinic for treatment, neutering was the top priority. Halt the chronic proliferation. With no leash laws nor raised eyebrows at the sight of stray cats or dogs roaming through the village, neighborhood animals whooped it up indiscriminately and often, the females routinely dropping slick litters of purple-lidded newborns onto grassy patches in back yards.

Wendy ushered me to the mosaic-top table and poured tea. "Time to talk about your work arrangement," she said, handing me a pad of paper. I'd want to take plenty of notes. Her beloved menagerie was being entrusted in my care.

"Every morning at seven o'clock, Luciana arrives," Wendy began. "She doesn't have a key to the property gates, so you'll need to let her in..." Luciana was paid to clean cages and kennels and haul fifty-pound bags of dog and cat food from the market to the shelter's storage room. "After walking the dogs, you'll fill their food and water bowls, oh, and fill them both morning *and* evening, please." Wendy set her cup on the tabletop, her bangle bracelets clinking against the mosaic stone. She fluffed her chin-length, product-blonde hair. "The dogs should get brushed every day. With the heat and the sand, some get quite matted." I'd also need to give the tortoises their daily platter of leafy greens and tomatoes, assist the veterinarian when asked and wouldn't it be nice if I could complete a project or two, like clearing stones and chipped bricks from the side yard and driveway.

Wendy leaned toward me and lowered her voice. "I know it's a bit overboard," she confided, propping her clasped hands under her chin. "But I feed Chiripa by hand."

Chiripa was a 17-year-old Dachshund, the size of a football, with arthritic knuckles and crinkly, hairless black ears – toughened flaps of leathery cartilage resembling an iron burn on a white shirt. Wendy unfolded her hands facing her palms skyward. Her tone of voice raised from sultry to tight. "Luciana assures me that if Chiripa got hungry enough, she'd eat on her own." Her bosom heaved a sigh. "I'm sure she's right. My little sausage dog would eat." Chiripa glanced up, her wet eyes rimmed in black skin tags. "I worry she won't eat enough…"

Chiripa clicked across the patio in the direction of the wicker dog baskets lined against the kitchen cottage's exterior wall. Three other dogs – Daisy, a three-legged border collie; King, a fatty tumored mutt; and Rosie, a silky-tailed Irish Setter mix – lounged in their baskets in the shade.

Rosie opened her mouth in a yawn. She was a beautiful dog. Strawberry blonde fur, long-legged, lithe. Chiripa moved on instinct in a beeline toward the shaded dog beds, tripping over the water bowl and head-bumping into a table leg on her way. The other dogs raised their heads slightly, letting out huffs of air as if to say, *Oh, fuck. Here it comes again.*

Reaching her final destination, Chiripa knocked into the side of Rosie's basket with her snout.

"Grrrrr!"

"Rosie! That's enough!" Wendy warned. Resigned, Rosie stood slowly and stretched forepaws onto rough patio bricks as Chiripa squeezed in to occupy the basket, plopping on her side, a contented sack of bones.

"Feed Chiripa twice a day," Wendy continued, "the special canned food, along with whisked milk and egg..."

I looked at Chiripa who slept curled, her gnarled wrists and ankles bent at ninety-degree angles, her water-balloon belly rising and falling with each sporadic breath. I knew that, for the next five weeks, my top job was keeping Chiripa alive.

*

It was my first time holding a male down by his thighs while another woman ripped his balls out, so I was surprised when the veterinarian told me I was a natural at it.

"Excellente," Dr. Alvarez said. I pressed the flat of my middle fingers firmly on the fine, sweat-slicked fur on the insides of the kitten's legs.

The kitten had been anaesthetized yet released a high-pitched yelp when Dr. Alvarez pulled the kitty testicle up and away from its scrotal sac. "Ay!" I whispered, glancing at the floor. With a quick clamp at the base of the spermatic cord followed by a firm tug, the testis – like a tiny balloon the color of a blood blister, with squiggly string attached – was released.

After the clamp and pluck surgery was completed, Dr. Alvarez pointed towards a produce box in the corner of the room. "Kitten orphans," she said. The newborns had been abandoned, left on their own to starve. "Feed every two hours," Dr. Alvarez instructed, handing me a plastic bottle along with a swaddling towel for each kitten. The veterinary intern was responsible for most feedings, but I was to take a few shifts per day until the kittens could gum something harder than a rubber nipple and ingest solid food. I'd envisioned a clan of silky-whiskered, pink-pawed babies. I removed the lid from the box to find five mewing fresh-out-of-the-placenta, crusty-eyed felines. Cradling the first kitten in my palm, I touched the nipple to its lips. Rather than latching on, it moved its head and limbs in robotic motion, hissing at shadows, pawing at air.

Each morning Luciana arrived at seven o'clock sharp wearing, over her T-shirt, a black mesh, Velcro-strapped back brace. "Buenos Dias," she said and moved into action dishing out dog food, cleaning cat cages, scooping up after canine lawn-shitters.

This was my cue to start walking dogs which I did, leading two at a time down Niebla's dirt roads lined with one-story box houses, painted in blues and yellows, with Direct TV dishes affixed like tipped haloes.

The dog I saved for last, walking her alone, was Pinky, the Peruvian Inca Orchid -- a completely hairless, eighty-pound powerhouse of a dog with flesh the peach-beige color of a hallway in a psych ward.

Pinky wore a navy-blue wool cape of sorts, like an open cardigan sweater, to block the sun's intense rays from her bare shoulders and upper back. Each morning after our walk I smoothed sunblock along her lower back, haunches and forelegs knobbed with scaly elbows. The landscape of her body felt perfectly human until I reached her paws and tail. The flesh of her rump, exposed to sun and regardless of the sunblock, was leathery and wart-smattered and stood in sharp contrast to the clear, supple skin underneath her wrap.

It all felt a bit ridiculous walking Pinky through town, pantsless and donned in her cape, while she hard-tugged at her leash ahead of me. I tried not to stare at the view immediately before me -- basically a middle-aged woman's bare ass. A well-toned ass, but still.

Pinky made a break for it one afternoon, while I lingered in the nearby town of Calida. I was grocery shopping in Calida's cinderblock-walled marketplace, stepping over mango peels and scraps of raw chicken fat, weaving through tables of farmer's produce. Green chilis, Habaneros, Poblanos piled on one table. White corn and ripe tomatoes on the next. I pressed my thumb against the skin of an avocado. A gentleman said, "Buenas tardes." I'd noticed him glancing my way earlier at the peppers table.

"Buenas tardes," I responded and the game began.

He inquired about my nationality, my work, mi familia. He smiled. "No esposo?" He was wearing a short-sleeve button-down shirt. Muscular arms.

"No esposo," I confirmed. I asked about his work, his hobbies, his family. Widower, he told me. I nodded slowly as he recommended a café nearby. He tilted his head, lifted his chin. Strong neck. The café was a quiet place, he continued. Good coffee. Tasty Churros. He'd love to hear about my work with the animales.

Suddenly, I felt caught off guard. When was the last time I washed my hair? Did my T-shirt smell? I hadn't brought lip gloss. Were my lips peeling? The cafe sounds nice, I told him but, sadly, I needed to get back. There were kittens to tend to, tortoises to feed. Perhaps another day, I added. I shopped here often.

Meanwhile, Pinky had been digging at the packed sand beneath her kennel fence, tunneling her escape route. By the time I arrived back at the animal rescue center, Pinky's kennel was empty. I searched the property. No Pinky. Most likely, she was hightailing it – caped and bare-assed -- through the dusty town of Niebla.

Rattling a bowl of dry dog food, I called for her. "Pinky! Pinky?" Rushing down unpaved streets, I ducked into vendor huts. "Has visto a mi perro?" Have you seen my dog? They shrugged. "Mi perro?" My dog? I pressed. Have you seen a big, naked dog running free? No, was their answer, again and again. I searched the shoreline, running past weathered, one-story houses that lay like flattened shoeboxes, their porches propped on timber stilts waiting for high tide. "Pinky?" I ran past houses where owners posted handwritten cardboard signs -- *Se cura picadura de raya*. They had *se cura*, the cure, in case a swimmer bounded into the water and inadvertently stepped on one of the stingrays that bottom-fed along the shallow shore. These good Samaritans with se cura would rush out, remove the spiny, venomous barb that had been tail-whipped into the swimmer's heel, sole or ankle. They'd suction the venom from the punctured foot and send the swimmer off to a medical clinic. The stingray would glide off toward a coral reef, the black lines of its gills and plate-mouth drawn on its white underbelly like the face of a smiling ghost.

"Pinky! Pinky?"

She was nowhere to be found. Perhaps Pinky would return home on her own after her legs grew tired from fleeing. When her stomach began aching for familiar food and her body craved the soft blanket in her kennel. When her heart hungered for companionship. I walked back home to make dinner with the vegetables and chicken I'd bought at the market. But my stomach churned sour, my appetite lost.

To be Peruvian seemed to require patience. Standing in stalled lines at the Western Union window. Wishing your water and electric would come back on. Waiting for buses and colectivos; hoping there'd be room for one more.

I sensed an attitude in Niebla -- We have nothing but time. The afternoon I heard Rosie's "Grrrrr!" as Chiripa meandered near her food bowl, I feared Chiripa's time was running out.

"Rosie, no!" I yelled. My reprimand wasn't fair. After all, it *was* Rosie's food. As if struck by a nervous tick, Rosie swung her head to the side in a shot, biting Chiripa's ribcage.

"No!" In a frenzy, Chiripa scurried toward my voice. Rosie returned to her bowl, devouring dry nuggets containing "real beef and egg." *Grrrrr.*

Chiripa's wound was shallow -- an inch-long section of exposed pinkish-red flesh, easily doctored with water and antibiotic ointment. The wound would heal quickly enough. It was Chiripa's spiking stress level from the trauma that concerned me, her heart the size of a baby's fist thumping beneath her ribs. "It's okay," I reassured, stroking her bony spine -- a carnal string of rosary beads. Chiripa leaned against my leg, alligator-mouthed and panting.

In the veterinary cottage, I set Chiripa's pillowed basket beside me, surveying her state of well-being while I fed kittens. Cradling a gray, white-pawed kitten, I touched the bottle nipple to its lips. "Open up," I coaxed. The kitten opened its mouth to hiss and I inserted the nipple. A drop of milk landed on its tongue before the kitten twisted its head away from the bottle. "Let's try again." I dabbed the nipple to its lips. "Come on, little guy. You can do it." The kitten hissed, turned its head. At times, I wanted to squirt the milk into their mouths, force them to ingest what they needed to survive. Squirting the bottled milk, however, was out of the question. They could inhale fluid into their lungs, drown on the milk. All I could do was gently encourage parted lips and unclenched jaws and offer nourishment. Latching on was up to the kitten. Most times, they remained close-mouthed, batting their tiny paws, with claws thin as a fish bone, at the bottle.

If only the good Samaritans who lived along the shoreline had se cura for these orphaned kittens, se cura for my traumatized Chiripa, se cura for an eighty-pound, hairless dog who'd lost her way.

Two days after Pinky escaped, I heard rustling outside the front gate. Heavy breathing. It was early morning, just after sunrise, before Luciana arrived for her morning work shift. I cracked open the gate to find the caped wonder seated and panting. "Pinky!" I'm SO relieved you're here! SO happy that you're safe and sound. We'll celebrate, you and me. I'll roast a chicken tonight and give you the dark meat. "Come here, girl." I'll put a big scoop of canned Purina on top of your dry food. Bought two cans of Purina Beef and Gravy just for you. A DOLLAR per CAN. A DOLLAR for a can of DOG FOOD. Highway robbery, but it's worth every penny to have you back home.

When Luciana arrived that morning, she opened the door to Wendy's bedroom, the room where Chiripa slept, to find the usual – piss and dog shit puddled and smeared across the tile floor. "Ay! Pequeno cabron!" Luciana yelled.

Chiripa bolted outside, racing down two cement steps like a flying monkey to escape Luciana's broom.

My heart stopped and I prayed Chiripa's wouldn't.

"Chiripa!" I called. Kneeling, I extended my hand, feigning an offering of a savory scrap. "Chiripa," I sang. "Come to me, sweet girl." While I understood Luciana's frustration, my heart ached for the little sausage dog, abandoned by her beloved

Wendy for five weeks and left in the care of a stranger. Perhaps Chiripa lost control of her bladder and bowels at night due to old age. More likely, it was lack of discipline, simple bad manners. "Chiripa! Come!" I didn't have any food, but how would she know? She turned toward my voice, padding in my direction, bumping into a shrub and teetering between the row of bricks lining the walkway. A wind-up toy in a maze.

At Calida's marketplace, I wove my way from tables of squash to asparagus to sweet potatoes. On the other side of the market, the gentleman I'd spoken with a few days earlier was there shopping. The man who'd invited me to a café for sweet talk and Churros. The man with the strong neck. That day, I was prepared. My hair was washed, my shirt clean, my lips glossed. I watched him from across the cavernous marketplace. He seemed to be bargaining with a vendor over the price of poultry. Money was exchanged. Raw chicken slid into a sack. I breathed in, ready to make my move. The gentleman moved toward another vendor, his back turned to me. I watched him walk, his knees bowing out a bit, his ankles rolling in, his hip flexors stiff. Was that a limp? I bit my lip. How old was this guy? When we'd stood face-to-face, flirting across the produce table, I'd guessed he might be inching toward sixty. Watching him in motion from behind, from the waist down, was he closer to seventy? Jesus. When had I become part of that romance market demographic? How many years before my dating game flipped from the role of seductive nurse to geriatric nurse?

I slipped quietly out of the marketplace. Took a roundabout route to the lot where colectivos waited. Back at Wendy's, I sat in the veterinary cottage, offering kittens words of consolation. "That's okay, little fella." It all seemed so unfair.

They'd gone through the effort, in utero, to split cells and grow a heart only to pass through the birth canal and be abandoned from day one. "You have to get stronger," I whispered, losing patience with their fragility, my inability to help. I gazed down at the kittens sleeping piled, a mound of furry bodies lying limp as beanbags, spiraling toward failure to thrive. Over the following few days, one kitten took its final breath, then another, and another, their souls released, floated, free.

On my final day in Peru, I sat on the floor of Wendy's bedroom offering Chiripa a handful of canned dog food mixed with milk and whisked raw egg. "Bueno, mi Chiripa." Chiripa chewed open-mouthed. "Good little eater."

For five weeks, I'd prepared and fed Chiripa special food, cajoled her into her dog bed in Wendy's room for afternoon naps and ten o'clock bedtimes. I'd followed her around the yard, assessing potential hazards like concrete steps, menacing dogs, heat exhaustion, convinced of her feebleness.

Yet for the latter part of her roughly one hundred and twenty dog years, Chiripa had opened her eyes each morning, mustering up enough energy to climb out of her basket and wander around Wendy's room shitting and pissing and running scared from her own flatulence. Through a fog of cataracts, she'd navigated her way through the yard each day, lifting her snout to whiff cat pheromones and turn her face to the sun. Some days she'd lumber about, fatigued. Other days she'd wag her tail while trailing a cricket in the grass or pedal a hind leg as I scratched her belly. Isn't this what we're all aiming for? To warm hearts when we enter a room? To lift spirits by simply being there? To persist with tenacity? To make it to something that old someday? To something that dear?

"Bueno, mi Chiripa." Wendy's beloved sausage dog chewed a mouthful of food, gelatinous chunks of imitation meat. "Atta girl."

It was around one o'clock, and I had a long day of travel ahead. I'd catch a colectivo to Calida, then make bus connections headed south. I needed to get on the road. My Peruvian visa expired soon. Wendy and I had discussed arrangements for covering Chiripa's care on my last day. The changing of the guards. Wendy would arrive home by early evening, and Luciana was scheduled to care for the animals later that afternoon. The odds seemed in our favor that, over the next few hours, Chiripa wouldn't be bitten or tripped over or hollered into cardiac arrest. She'd make it until Wendy got home. My work was done.

I strapped on my dense backpack leaning forward then bouncing it higher onto my back like a parent propping a child piggyback. Stepping through the front gate, I walked along a still, side road. The sandy streets and yards of Niebla created the air of a dusty frontier town. It was December. At the four-corners I passed a towering cone wire construct girdled with cedar fur boughs – a part real, part fake Christmas tree – its steel trunk bored solid into the ground. The green boughs were bandaged with wide, decorative silver ribbon dotted with ball ornaments, a red-fringed star sat on top. The tree stood straight and alone, a thin blanket wrapped around its metal trunk.

On the covered patio of a nearby home, a woman flapped a rectangle of pink satin cloth over a folding table, smoothing wrinkles from the fabric before setting stacks of plastic cups and paper plates on the table's surface. A birthday cake, with blue and white waved ribbons of icing was placed in the center, along with a rainbow striped llama piñata. Later, at this home, children would giggle, shriek, eat cake served in wedges. They'd dance, to hard-beat music blared through car speakers, on this patio decorated with tissue flowerets and balloons.

"Mama!" a thin-legged girl in a ruffled magenta dress called out. "Tengo globos!" She held a bouquet of balloons, her fingers curled in a fist around the ribbon ties. The balloons – yellows, reds, and blues – bobbed together and apart like a crowd of mingling party goers.

"Ay!" The girl gasped. A blood red birthday balloon escaped from the bunch, as balloons do, and was released, its string squiggling through the air, liberated into clear sky.

I walked to the beach where colectivos typically parked, waiting. The tidewater was rising -- exhale, hold, exhale, hold – reminding me of that day after school when our backyard creek swelled. Flooded in a flash. Soon after I'd attempted to save the drowning plants, my mother had brought home new cardboard flats of tomato, pepper and cucumber seedlings to replace the carnage. I'd knelt in the dirt, digging holes, setting root balls in soil. With my index and middle fingers, I'd pressed the dirt around their stalks, tucking them in, hoping the universe might offer up a long growing season. Give them more time. In a small section of the garden, we'd re-planted some of the seedlings I'd pulled in a panic from the earth. Most remained wilted, their leaves yellowing, withering, their roots unable or unwilling to latch on. One of them, a tomato plant, had defied the odds, stretched its roots into moist soil, its leaves perked and green, reaching skyward to face the sun.

I walked toward the colectivos, my sandals digging into sand. How many days remained in Chiripa's growing season? A hundred maybe? More or less? I watched the tidewater roll in, filling holes that children had dug with their small hands and plastic shovels. Gently sweeping away sand dollars broken in halves, strands of seaweed, fanned algae, my footprints in the sand.

Goat Nature

In my father's farmhouse in upstate New York, near a painted sign which reads, *Barker's Horse Liniment – Good for Mules and Jackasses*, hangs my favorite photograph. In that framed photo my father, about thirty years old, is kneeling in barn straw surrounded by baby goats. The goats are nuzzling his face, climbing his shoulder, sucking his ear lobe. My father's smiling, handsome, seemingly unbreakable. Like the corporal in a war drama who always made it out alive.

While traveling, I checked in with my father regularly. He enjoyed hearing about my experiences overseas. What are your students like in South Korea? He'd wanted to know. How many orphans are you taking care of in Ethiopia? Will the shelter animals in Peru find homes? When I left Peru and began my month-long volunteer gig working at a goat farm in Fuerteventura, Spain, he was eager for me to share the details.

One Sunday afternoon, after a morning of sweeping pens and suctioning 700 goat teats, I called my father.

"You say they have over three hundred goats there?" he'd asked.

"More like three-fifty," I'd said.

"So, you're not milking by hand then."

"Oh, no. It's high tech."

"All the goats are free ranged?"

"Yeah. They have a good life. The farm must have over a hundred acres..."

"Well, I'll be darned," he'd said. "Sounds like fun."

I'd thought it would be fun, too. I'd discovered the goat farm on a work exchange website. The posted headline read, *Volunteer in Sunny Fuerteventura!* Beneath that was a photograph of a woman cradling a baby goat, its bowed head made heavy by long velveteen ears. The kind you see in Hush Puppy ads. *Free room and board in exchange for chores on our family-run goat farm.* Private room with separate entrance and adjoining bath. Home-cooked meals at a family dinner table. A backpacker's heaven.

For the first three months or so of backpacking, I felt energized by the adventure. Then fatigue began boring its way in. I was tired of sharing sleeping quarters in cheap hostels with late night pot smokers, sick of hand-washing my bra and dirty jeans in a bucket. The farm family might let me use their washing machine. My head swooned.

I sent a carefully worded email touting my reliability, positivity, and love for all things bovid and landed a Skype interview with Ingrid, longtime girlfriend of one of the grown sons, Victor. "Veektor," she pronounced it. "You're an English teacher!" Ingrid beamed. Victor and Ingrid didn't live on the Canary Island of Fuerteventura – a 60-mile-long and 20-mile-wide expanse of gray bedrock dotted with coarse, prickly vegetation. They lived in Madrid and were involved with the farm remotely. Their homebodied family members carried out day-to-day grange operations content to live on an island girdled in by goats.

The farm produced goat cheese, majorero, which sold well on the island and roused in Ingrid and Victor grand visions of international expansion. This meant the rest of the family needed to up their English skills to help sell their majorero globally. "English lessons," Ingrid said. "They might not take to the idea right away, but this will be so good for them."

Ingrid explained that I might need to help out with a light farm chore or two during my stay. My main job, however, would be helping the family with their English. Our Skype connection turned poor. Ingrid's face froze and pixilated halfway through the sentence, making her appear as if she'd been chewing on a ham sandwich then looked up to see a tidal wave coming her way.

Ingrid wouldn't be on the farm while I was there, she told me. Victor would show up sporadically. No worries, Ingrid assured me. Victor's amiable and gregarious family loved having volunteers. They'd show me the ropes. I'd teach some English, practice my Spanish, frolic with goats along scenic hilltops. Like Heidi, only thirty years older and without the braids.

The website included a family photo -- a man and woman in their sixties, their two grown sons, and their daughter balancing a toddler on her hip the way a potato farmer might carry a load. Each had cowbird-brown hair and the kind of radiant complexion achieved by drinking olive oil by the pint.

Standing in the bus station in Puerto del Rosario, I spotted the clan immediately. Ingrid knew full well that I was a middle-aged teacher on hiatus, rather than your typical, college-aged volunteer. Judging from the *What the fuck?* expression on the family members' faces when I approached them and introduced myself, that bit of information hadn't been passed on. They slid open the door of their VW van with a roll of their eyes and a shrug of their shoulders.

The van snaked along a quiet road, eventually turning onto the long, gravel driveway to the farm. With its stately house surrounded by a vast expanse of land, it was more like a ranch, a Bonanza, a place you'd expect to find gauchos on horseback or Hoss eating a charbroiled Ribeye stabbed on a fork.

Meals at the goat farm took place in the family's cavernous, ceramic-tiled and wood-beamed kitchen. A room straight off the pages of *Better Homes and Gardens* or *My Spanish Kitchen is Better than Yours.* The midday meal was served at 2:30 p.m. by Madre who ladled meaty stew, in farmhand portions, into earthenware bowls. My Spanish was functional. I could chat about work, daily routine, family, hobbies. On a good day, I could understand about half of the dining table conversation.

"Por favor," Madre said, pointing to plates layered with prosciutto, green olives, crusty bread. The family of Spaniards, including Madre's five-year-old granddaughter, Camila, spoke circles around me. Occasionally, they paused to ask me a beginner-level-Spanish question. *Is the food good?* They projected loudly, slowly. Did they think I'd recently suffered a brain injury? "Si! Muy rico!" I'd respond. They'd smile wide-eyed, like a new parent hearing *Da Da* for the first time, then resume their conversation. A string of rapid-fire heartfelt vowels and rolling r's.

From the other room a television droned, a man's voice mumbled in growls. Halfway through the meal, I heard the rustling of a newspaper then feet shuffling. Padre appeared in sweatpants and bathrobe. He stomped his slipper-clad feet. Whimpered and tugged at his black hair. Something was off with him, like the faint smell of gas in an apartment building. Dementia, perhaps? Chronic pain? Madre retrieved a scone from the kitchen counter, tenderly pressed it into Padre's palm.

"Aqui mi amor." She led him back to the television. "Todo esta bien."

Victor's sister, Fabiana, turned toward me. "No hay leccion de ingles esta noche." Since it was my first night on the farm, she'd informed me, I didn't have to teach an English lesson. She gave me the once over with cold eyes.

Fabiana sliced a wedge of goat cheese and pointed to the prosciutto at the end of the table. "Pasar el plato." Madre passed the plate. Camila, Fabiana's daughter, tapped her empty cup against the tabletop. Madre filled it with milk. "You should get to bed early," Fabiana said. Morning milking began at six-thirty sharp. Madre turned to me, speaking slowly. I'd be milking with Oscar, her oldest son, she explained. Her other son, who sometimes helped with milking, was in Madrid. Fabiana tipped her empty bowl toward Madre. "Mama." Madre ladled stew into the bowl. After milking the goats, Madre said, she'd make me a big breakfast.

Just me and Oscar milking 350 goats while Fabiana, what, slept in? Ate breakfast in bed? On my father's farm, everyone pitched in. If a boy could muck a horse stall, throw a bale of hay, so could a girl. We saw value in getting our hands dirty. I glanced at Fabiana. There was something so petite-nosed and coif-browed about her. So twig-armed and big-boobed. A Spanish Barbie doll. I gave Madre a warm smile. "Morning milking," I began. "No Fabiana?" Fabiana narrowed her Barbie doll eyes.

At 6:15 a.m. I entered the milking barn, an aluminum-sided building situated a bocce ball roll away from the house. Oscar was there, flipping on switches, checking hoses and connections. He was a hardworking man of few words with thick, wavy hair, strong shoulders, and hands the size of pita bread. "Buenos dias, Oscar." Glancing at my sneakers, he pointed to rubber boots lined near the door and motioned for me to follow him. I clomped outside in oversized boots heading toward the back of the barn. Oscar pointed at pastureland in the distance, held his flattened palm up, signaling "stop." He disappeared into the barn.

Next to a doghouse nearby, hunkered a blocky meathead of a mutt with the kind, muddied eyes of an old priest. "Hey, fella." The dog leaned into his collar, which was clipped to a short chain of fat, metal loops. He barked out a string of throaty howls. I inched toward him. "It's okay, Handsome." His beefy tail thumped the ground. I scratched his ears, rubbed his neck. "That feels good, doesn't it, Senor Guapo?" His back paw pedaled. "Such a good dog…"

"Oye!" Oscar bellowed. "Cabras!"

I looked up to see a herd of goats running across the pasture and storming the barn. Most entered the holding area to await milking. A dozen had gone rogue, straying from the herd. They were face-deep in vegetation. "Oye!" Oscar shooed the weed-eating goats toward the barn's pen, flailing his hands in my direction. Apparently, running interference between goats and weeds was my job. Oscar secured the goats in the holding pen. "Vamos!" I slogged in my giant rubber boots, trying to catch up. Clown feet.

Oscar gestured toward a stack of 40-pound bags of pellets and corn. I was to lift them, empty their contents into troughs. Oscar spoke no English. Only pointed, waved, flailed, gesticulated. A farmer mime. My charge was to distribute the feed evenly along the fifty-foot trough. Oscar eyed my handiwork and grimaced. I slunk down the five grated metal steps to get into position for milking.

The upper level of the milking barn held feeding cribs and metal partitioned parlor stanchions. The lower level contained a row of suction devices with yards of tubing that fed into a 500-gallon stainless-steel tank which appeared icy and slick. Laboratorial.

Oscar slid the barn door open and the first group of 40 nannies spilled in. They scrambled to their larder in a craze. In the goats' single-mindedness to get first dibs on the corn and pellets, they scarcely noticed Oscar shooing them into their stanchions – hind quarters facing the lower level – then slapping down the metal bar to lock their heads in place.

Goats' short tails curl up exposing *everything*. Oscar and I stood eye-level with 40 nanny buttholes and twice as many nipples. I followed Oscar's lead. Slid suction cones onto the pair of teats in front of me. Monitored milk flow through the clear tubing. When a stream of milk tapered to dribbles, I scrunched the skin of the nanny's udder. Coaxed the machine to suck her dry. Life on a goat farm. Not exactly what I'd imagined. Where was the gentle fellow in dungarees? Who sat on a wooden stool, a silver bucket at his feet, gently massaging milk from his untethered goat, Lucy?

*

I'd found Oscar rather attractive until I saw the way he handled teats. He bore the daily responsibility of milking hundreds of goats in a time-efficient manner. No room for foreplay. When Oscar approached each nanny, her bony hind legs kicked out from side to side like a folk dancer on speed. He thrusted his hands between her limbs, grasped the long pink nipples and tugged down with a twist. Like a sausage maker having a bad day.

While I enjoyed a surprise or two in the bedroom, the eye-opener I encountered my first night on the farm left a lot to be desired. In my pajamas, I padded across the chilled tile floor, slid under the top sheet and comforter, and turned off the light. What the hell? What felt like mini electric shocks, the voltage an undisciplined lab mouse might receive from a corrective collar, zapped my body. The zinging targeted my armpits and groin then the crease in my belly. I wasn't in bed alone.

Three hundred and fifty goats meant thousands of fleas. In the light of the following morning, I saw fleas everywhere. In my socks, jacket sleeves, the cups of my bra. I stepped from the shower and they hopped from the bathmat onto my feet. The hard plated boingers vaulted from my backpack to the bed. Each morning before milking, I shook out my blanket, sheets, and clothes. The short-spined bastards held their territory. When captured, I rolled and crushed them between my fingers, pressed their armored bodies against the floor until motionless. Each night I lay in bed, like a dental patient waiting for the pinch of Novocain. I awakened exhausted. Dots of dried blood peppering my bedsheets.

When I'd first agreed to volunteer at the goat farm, Victor told me that I'd have Sunday afternoons off. On my first Sunday there, after morning milking rounds, pinning the family's wet laundry on clothes lines, sweeping porches, and feeding goats, I walked two miles to a café. The nearest public spot with Wi-Fi.

I opened my computer. My friend, Tina, had emailed from Rochester. Vented about her local grocer's dismal selection of tomatoes and peppers. Asked if I'd heard about the Spanish vole infestation. My father had written. His horse, Stanley, was lame again. The farrier was coming out that day. In the meantime, he'd soak his hoof.

There was a time my father had twelve horses, some cows, chickens, dogs and cats, a goose. Years passed. His shoulders narrowed. Hair thinned. The skin over his triceps slacked a bit. He began looking at each porch step before setting down his boot.

By the time he turned seventy, he'd downsized to five horses, a few scruffy barn cats and a dog. My father remained ruggedly handsome. Able-bodied. Occasionally, he cleaned up for weddings, baptisms, appearing manly elegant in light gray slacks and suit jacket. His everyday clothes were bought at the Salvation Army and worn until threadbare. Jeans with frayed hems. T-shirts with oil stains. A knit cap chewed through by mice. Put Clint Eastwood and a rabid badger in a burlap bag for an hour. What would crawl out would be my father saying, "You should see the badger."

My father was in his mid-seventies when I stayed with him for ten days after his hip replacement surgery. The year before that, he underwent radiation for prostate cancer. Before that, the dentist pulled his existing teeth, replacing them with a full plate of dentures. *New teeth in 2011. Glowing prostate in 2013. Brand new hip this year! Ladies, what are you waiting for?*

The surgeon who replaced my father's hip estimated a three-day hospital stay. My check list: *Teach final class of semester. Fly up north. Bring father home from hospital. Help with recovery.*

Forty-eight hours after my father's surgery, I pulled my rental car into his driveway. He was standing on the porch, leaning ever so slightly on his hospital issued walker. I said, "I thought your discharge was tomorrow."

He smiled. "They wanted to keep me for three days because I live alone. I told them I live with Marley." I rolled my eyes. Marley was his dog.

"Maybe we should head indoors," I said. "Get you comfortable. When was the last time you ate?"

"Huh?" My father, a retired audiologist, by his own admission *can't hear for shit.*

I strained my voice. "Indoors. Sit down. You hungry?"

"Okay."

The house air felt thick, and smelled of dust, dog fur and open-can cat food. I entered his bathroom. Beneath the windowsill, scores of dead Lady bugs lay piled, their tiny, stiffened legs folded flat beneath dried tomato-red shells with happy black polka dots. Tomb mounds.

My father sat in his recliner. Leaned back a notch. Velcro strap sneakers propped and raised. I mentioned the Lady bugs.

"Huh?"

"Lady bugs."

"Those are probably their cousins, the Asian Lady Beetle," he told me.

I made fried bologna sandwiches. Set a bag of chips in his lap. Popped a beer tab and asked, "Want one?"

"One beer won't hurt."

I prompted a story. "Didn't you break your jaw a while back?"

He had. It happened while riding his horse, Peaches, cross country. Bareback, they galloped through field grass. He jumped her over a felled log. "I was jumping a felled log," my father said, "and I felled off."

After the fall, he'd remounted Peaches and rode home not thinking much of it. "Weren't you in a lot of pain?" I asked.

"It hurt," he acknowledged. "I just thought *Well, it hurts.*" A colleague looked at my father's lopsided face and told him, Get your ass to a doctor.

Before bed, my father unpacked the hospital-issue aluminum rod with plastic gripping apparatus. It was helpful for carrying out tasks such as picking up a piece of junk mail. *Do not bend* was the cardinal rule after hip replacement surgery. You could climb stairs. Walk around. But flex your hip more than a ninety-degree angle? The ball of your new hip implant could pop out of its socket. My father was using it to remove his socks and shoes.

"Piece of shit pole," he said, trying to pinch the top of his left sock then peel it down. He'd un-Velcroed his sneakers easily enough. Managed to shed his blue jeans that hung loose just below his hip bones. Standing in his living room in a T-shirt and Fruit of the Loom underwear, he was down to the socks. "The grippers just don't grab…"

I cleared my throat. "Would you like some help or are you feeling determined?"

He'd taken out his teeth by then. His mouth puckered in concentration. A drawstring sack pulled tight. "I'm determined." He pinched the neck of the sock with the gripper, pushed down, repositioned. Pinch. Push. Reposition.

I watched, fascinated. *Was this what it was like for Jane Goodall the first time she saw apes fish termites out of the ground with a stick?*

Five minutes and one bare foot later, he beamed. "Once you get it over the heel, it's a piece of cake."

I deluged my father with cautionary tales. Horror stories. "My friend Kathy had a great uncle who overdid things after his hip surgery," I warned. "Popped it right out." My father gave a blank look. I added, "That couldn't have been fun."

"Doesn't sound like it would be," he agreed. "Luckily, I have two hips." He planted his right foot firmly on the floor, extended his left leg behind him, stretched his arm forward, bent at the waist and picked up a fallen dish towel. Remember the glass bulb birds that, prompted by evaporation, lowered their beaks into a glass of water? Dippy Bird.

My father's approach to physical therapy: If the doctor suggests ten hip abduction exercises, do thirty. Ten quadriceps sets for ten minutes? Do twenty for twenty minutes. "I figure from here to the end of the living room is fifty-five feet," my father explained. "Fifty-two hundred and eighty feet make up a mile. If I walk back and forth fifty times, I've gotten in a little over a mile. Aiming for two."

That night my father's pain grew intense, unremitting. He couldn't sleep. The physical therapist arrived for a house visit the next morning. Checked his surgical site incision. My father described his exercise regime. She listened patiently. What do you recommend for his pain? I asked.

Her answer -- that he learn to sit the fuck down and stay there.

The following day, my father sat in his recliner, an ice pack wedged against his left hip. His dog rested its muzzle on the chair's arm. "Marley, come on up." Marley maneuvered his bulk onto my father's lap. "That's a good boy."

My father's forehead was damp. "You're sweating," I said. "Should we check your temperature?"

No need, he told me. He'd just finished extra sets of straight leg raises. "At first, I thought I really should tone the exercise down," he said. "But ice helps a lot."

He resumed his two-mile treks through the living room and kitchen, into the mud room and back again. Past the dog food bowls, the mini-fridge with beer, the wall-mounted wooden cross. My father walked back and forth through the house. Like a paddocked horse. One mile, then two. First with a walker, then a cane, then hands free. His lungs heaving. Longing for the outdoors where he could move free range.

His spirit, I knew was tough, but as I pulled my car out of his driveway, blowing goodbye kisses through my open window, I wondered, How much can a body can take?

*

English lessons at the goat farm were supposed to begin each night at seven-thirty. I sat alone at the dining room table listening to Padre throw tantrums in the other room. Oscar and Fabiana and her husband, Stephano, trickled in around eight o'clock. I wasn't sure where exactly Fabiana, Stephano and their daughter, Camila, lived, but it must have been nearby since they were at the farm most days, it seemed, for meals and socializing. Stephano knew some English. He wanted to work on sayings, he told me. Like bull in china room. "Ah, you want to learn idioms," I said. Yes, like kitchen pot say other pot black. I distributed the vocabulary sheets I'd handwritten sometime between feeding 700 pounds of alfalfa to the herd and damp mopping the living room. "Victor and Ingrid told me to teach English for selling goat cheese."

Collective huff.

Fabiana thumbed her dinging cell phone, cheering each time an Angry Bird saved an egg from a hungry green pig. Oscar disappeared into the TV room. He argued with Madre. My Spanish wasn't sophisticated enough to understand every detail of the conflict, but I made out enough words to understand that Oscar felt put upon. Madre wanted him to include me more.

"Por favor, Oscar," Madre pleaded. "Invite a la mujer mas a menudo." Invite the woman. In Madre's opinion, Oscar should have asked me to join the family for evening Sangria. And he should have included me when the cousins came to the house for cookies and beer.

I'd become accustomed to feeling excluded. One Saturday, when friends and relations swarmed the farm for a birthday party, Oscar gave me a wedge of chocolate hazelnut cake. Then handed me a mop to clean the cheese making room.

"Oscar, por favor. Invitala." Invite her. "Tratarla como a una familia." Treat her like family.

Oscar rejoined us in the kitchen. Sat at the table red-faced with annoyance. "Tonight," I began, holding up my worksheet, "let's form sentences using the words: *pasteurized*, *ounces*, *goat milk*, *custome*r and *mail order…*" I stood and circled the table, stopping to help Stephano with verb tenses, spelling English words for Oscar. When it came time to practice their sentences in a mock conversation, they simply read from their worksheets in monotone voices.

The following afternoon, Oscar pointed to his pickup truck. "Vamos." I looked at him quizzically. "Please," he added. We drove through pastureland, our elbows poking through open windows. Faces tilted toward sunshine. Oscar cleared his throat. "Me English," he said. "No good."

"Oh, Oscar. Es mucho mejor!" I told him. It's much better.

He grinned. The scratchy radio played the Rolling Stones. Jumpin' Jack Flash. "Deesko," Oscar said. Si! Disco! We bobbed our heads. Tapped our feet. Waved at farm workers digging irrigation channels in the soil. Comrades. We arrived at a small paddock area. Oscar opened the truck door for me. Gracias. He pointed to the goats in the paddock. There were about thirty of them. Juveniles. Roughly thirty-five pounds each. Gesturing toward a couple of particularly cute goats, Oscar said, Bonita. Patchwork brown, orange, black. Two-tone silver and white. Si! Bonita, I agreed. *How nice. He's giving me a tour of the farm.* Then he handed me a large plastic bottle -- Goat Dewormer -- and a bag of syringes. Medicina por las cabras. One by one, Oscar wrestled the goats. He shoved them into my arms. Blaaa! Blaaa! I gripped their bodies, squirming and kicking, while Oscar pried open their mouths, squirted dewormer under their tongues. Invite the woman. Treat her like family.

How did they do it? This family who ate goat cheese the size of tricycle wheels and slept in flea-lined bed sheets. Day after day. Chore after chore. How did they entertain their minds mundane task after task? I suppose they had a divine sense of purpose. It was their farm, business and family. Without that, I'd resorted to making up names for the goats. The nanny with the extra teat, I called Three. The goat missing a teat, Ace. There was Hair Bag and her polar opposite, Brazilian. And Crusty, Blinky, Lil Nips and Cannonballs. But for how long could that keep a healthy brain occupied?

The next morning, I entered the milking barn to find a cluster of day-old goats. Downy-lipped and weepy-eyed. Rounded bellies fixed with dried umbilical cords stiff as dead earthworms. The group meandered slow and dazed, like old men in pajamas.

The nanny goats spilled in. Oscar and I lifted the babies, who hung in our hands like sleepy kittens, and positioned them under the nannies to nurse. I expected them to target the obvious – the nannies' large pink sacks full of milk with nipples the size of Pez dispensers. Instead, they skittered under nanny armpits. Sucked on a kneecap or two. Then moved rearward.

Poked and prodded with wet noses. Finally, they made the connection. Teat! Latching onto the nipple, they jabbed at the udder, stimulating milk flow. The nannies defied maternal warmth. Head-clunked the babies with cleft hooves. *Get off me!* They seemed to say. *First Oscar, now you!*

In the milking barn, a baby emerged as pack leader of a half-dozen newborns. At one week old, she was long-legged and angular. Black-furred with a heart-shaped face. Her ears stuck straight out to the sides, like the Tasmanian Devil I'd seen in cartoons. She looked like something futuristic. I named her Space Racer.

"Come on, girl!" Space Racer followed me. Past the doghouse. Through the pasture. In the feeding barn, she nibbled my pant leg. Sucked on my finger. "Don't tell the others," I said, pulling cracked corn from my pocket and feeding her by hand.

No matter how earnestly a nanny tried to clunk Space Racer in the head, once she scored a teat, she locked on and held ground. She was dodgy and fearless. Unbreakable.

During a Skype chat with a friend in Rochester, New York, I made a mistake. "Milking the goats is okay," I told her. "The chore I *really hate* is weeding around olive trees."

"Olive trees! I'd give anything to be weeding in sunny Spain rather than freezing my ass off here. And it's only October! I'll probably be shoveling fucking snow next month..."

Friends often referred to my travels as an "adventure." The reality of farm work and language barrier, however, even in sunny Spain, felt isolating. I'd hoped to feel a sense of community on this family farm, a kinship. Instead, I remained outside the herd.

The next day, for three hours, I crouched and circled tree trunks inch by inch pulling weeds, their roots dried into hard soil.

It was over the olive tree weeding that I got into it with Fabiana. She knocked on my door in a Mediterranean huff one Sunday afternoon. I was about to walk to the café. Drink coffee. Check emails. Fabiana seemed to think I should be delighted to work non-stop seven days a week. What, with my regal accommodations and goat cheese consumption and all.

Fabiana stood pinch-faced, her tiny doll hands on hips. She pointed to me. Then to the olive trees. I yelled in bad Spanish, Sunday afternoon! No work. Veektor said! Fabiana snorted off like a feral hog to a hard-boiled egg.

I sensed a rumor spreading through the family that I should be working harder. From my perspective, I milked goats for four hours each morning, did crap for farm chores every afternoon except Sunday and taught English grammar and common phrases such as *How would you like your goat cheese sliced?* to a disinterested family of Spaniards most evenings. From their perspective, I should do more.

Who is this unmarried fifty-year-old woman who lives out of a backpack and forces us to study English vocabulary? Could that be what they were saying about me? *How the hell did she end up living on our goat farm?*

Shortly after I defied Fabiana's direct order, Victor showed up blinking and sweaty. There'd been a scheduling mix-up, he explained. The family needed me on the farm for four weeks, not five. He pressed his finger to a calendar. That day. Bye-bye.

Fine.

Goats will stare you down with their slit-pupiled eyes like goth band lead singers. In the feeding barn, I swept debris from troughs. Shoveled mounds of dung and straw. Two sides of the barn were unwalled, open to acreage for goats to wander. Most goats were out in the distance. A meandering collection of bovine, some with wattles and belled collars. I heaved a vacuum-packed nylon bag of pressed alfalfa into a wheelbarrow. Sliced the bag open with my razor. The goats thundered in, 350 strong, low blaaaing like Gyuto monks.

There's an oil painting housed in Museo Del Prado in Madrid. Painted around the year 1500. *The Garden of Earthly Delights.* One panel depicted Hell. In it, a bird-headed demon ate corpses. Naked humans were thrown into flames. They shat out coins. Vomited snakes. If that scene were sound tracked, it would resemble the noise of three hundred goats clamoring for food. Low-pitched grunts. High-pitched screams. The symphonic sonance of a day on a psychiatric ward.

I tore flakes of alfalfa from the bale. Tossed them into troughs. Tried to keep up with the craze. The goats seemed to think I wasn't working fast enough. They jumped over, squeezed under, side-slammed one another to get to alfalfa. "Relax," I told them. "I'm getting another bag…" The goats stared. *Tempus fugit.*

Once the stack of bales was depleted, the nannies moved out to roam their expanse of land. I moved into the adjacent barn to visit baby goats. Sliding my hands under the belly of a nut-brown newborn, I pulled him against me. "Hey there, cutie." Through the light of the open door, I noticed a lump outside in the distance.

On the sandy ground, the babe lay still. Sections of black fur appearing slightly stiff. She lay on her side, legs stretched out, like an old dog lying in the sun. Was she taking a rest from goat nature? From jumping, head butting, strategizing for teat. I neared. Saw her eyes clouded in milky grey. The red dabs of liquid crowning from black nostrils. The look of roadkill.

Kneeling beside Space Racer, I rubbed my hand along the top of her head. *You and those silly ears.* I traced her two nubs of horn. Like baby teeth coming through. *Look at those fuzzy little lips of yours.* Had her skull ached the way a baby's gums ache when teeth are coming in?

Had she tried to nurse on the wrong nanny? Received a deadly, enraged blow? Or was she crushed in the 350-goat frenzy to feed? *Sorry, baby girl.* A body can only take so much.

If there's such a thing as goat heaven, I imagine endless pasture rolled with mixed grasses and clover. Maybe a pond, a clear-watered brook. Scattered shelters padded with dry straw. Buckets brimming with corn and pumpkin seeds, raisins and grain. Tree stumps and hills and boulders for climbing. A felled log or two easily jumped.

No lungworm or hoof rot. No arthritis or abscesses. No branding irons. No predators. No Oscar.

My vision of heaven might miss the point. Is it truly paradise to live without the urge to follow instinct? To feel no driving force? To exist without the tension, the risk, the fight that reminds us of our wholehearted intention to survive?

I smoothed the black fur along Space Racer's neck. Stroked the soft coat above her ribcage. Traced her hip bone. Was it fragile? Did it hurt? Just the day before, Space Racer communed with her herd of stout-bodied nannies. Leading their Bambi-legged babes furred in patchworks of orange, brown and white. Navigating the pasture, its rocks and grasses. Bounding and head-butting, nuzzling and nestling. Blaaing away, just like family.

Trailing the Wrong Scent

After leaving the goat farm, I shook off my fleas and moved on to mainland Spain where I spent a week walking the cobblestone streets of Granada, pausing at basilicas and Islamic palaces and trekking unpaved roads past countryside homes and small farms with chickens and sheep.

During my backpacking year, on days I stayed in cheap hostels rather than volunteering for room and board, I'd curl up in the community room bean bag chair and take a hollow-cheeked drag of television. I'd sip morning coffee with CNN's Anderson Cooper. Drink a beer while watching a food truck show. If lucky, I'd run across the *Dog Whisperer,* featuring a plucky Mexican-American canine behaviorist named Cesar Millan. Episodes of *Dog Whisperer* showed exasperated canine owners dealing with dogs gone rogue. You might see, for example, a mother of three in tears as her Peek-a-Poo, Hannibal, terrorizes dinner guests. Or an accountant standing wide-eyed and stunned when his Weimaraner, Pixie, leaps onto the kitchen counter, devouring a rotisserie chicken. Cesar arrives on the scene -- *I train people and rehabilitate dogs* – flashing his calm, assertive energy and teeth the bright white of an Oxi-clean scrub. With a quick *Schht, Schht* from Cesar, the

Schnauzer that had chewed off the doll heads of five blonde Barbies lowers its muzzle. "First he smell me," Cesar says moving like a slow-motion Ninja toward the penitent canine. "Later he lick me." By episode's end, the same dog that'd exhibited the anxiety of a rabid raccoon lay sprawled and submissive, gazing at Cesar like a lovesick camel.

I had the television room to myself in my Granada hostel. Brushing Dorito crumbs from the inseam of my worn sweatpants, I leaned toward the televised image of Cesar in starched jeans and black T-shirt. "For those who don't know what breed am I," Cesar began, rubbing a hand through his silver Cockatiel hair. "I am Mexican."

Mexico. I'd lived in Asia, traveled in Africa, South America, Spain. Yet I hadn't spent much time in Mexico, my home country's neighbor. It was a country I was interested in learning more about. The Zocalo in Mexico City. Yucatan cenotes and wildlife. Waterfalls and gardens in the southern state of Chiapas. Since it was relatively close to home, perhaps I'd taken it for granted.

A week later, I was cleaning rooms at a hostel in Cordoba in exchange for room and board. After my work shift, I wandered through a local museum. *More Roman tombstones.* I yawned. *Another marble oscillum.* When had traveling become same old, same old? Maybe it was time to throw down my backpack. Drink water from a glass rather than plastic bottle. Earn a paycheck. Maybe it was time to wear normal pants again.

*

"Now that Alonzo at Headquarters has signed your employment contract," Rafael explained during our follow-up

Skype interview, "the next step is securing your work visa. It's a very simple process." Rafael was the proprietor of the language school, English Now!

I'd responded to an online ESL job site advertisement for a Director of Studies position. Once hired, I'd supervise a team of teachers, provide professional development workshops, coordinate class schedules. English Now! was in Mexico.

"After you arrive," Rafael continued, "we'll fill out the necessary paperwork to secure your visa."

"For past positions," I told him, "I received my work visa ahead of time."

"Really, it's no problem," Rafael replied. "You'll have a work contract with English Now! so as far as Mexican immigration is concerned, you're legitimate."

Through my computer screen, I studied Rafael who sat at his desk in white shirt, tie, and navy blazer. He was poised, polished and so fluent in English that you'd think he was from Denver.

I pressed him. "Immigration will be fine with a work contract rather than visa?"

"Listen, if you're worried about it, send a scan of every page in your passport and we'll get the ball rolling now."

I wanted the job. Director of Studies. A chance to make a decent living. Settle into a stable life again. In sunny Mexico!

"I'll send the scan today," I told him.

Rafael smiled. "Good." He chattered on about finding me an apartment within walking distance of the school. "There's a nice grocery store right down the road…a beautiful park nearby…" Then he added, "In the off chance that we don't get your work visa processed, when you talk with customs at the airport, make sure you say, 'tourist.'"

"But…"

"Just remember," Rafael repeated, "Tourist."

Three weeks later, I stood across from a Mexican Customs officer who glanced from my passport photo to my face. "What is your occupation?" he asked.

"I'm a teacher on hiatus," I said.

"Where will you be staying?" He rubbed a hand over his overgrown brush-cut.

I recited the address of the small hotel that Rafael had agreed to put me up in until I found an apartment.

"What are your plans here in Mexico?" he asked, holding a rubber stamp in his hand.

"I'm interested in sight-seeing," I said. It was true. I was interested in sight-seeing.

On my first day of work, Rafael led me through the school's cheerful, white adobe reception area, past a small courtyard with cacti, Ficus and Esperanza the color of lemon drops and into my tidy, sunny office. The physicality of the building, with its Cape blue window shutters and glassy, tile flooring felt all rainbows and puppy-breath. By the end of my first week, I'd met with all eight of our foreign English teachers. They filed, one by one, into my office, carrying with them the joy of a gray cloud.

Rafael, as proprietor of English Now!, needed to increase client numbers to keep the school running and prosperous. There was sizeable profit in providing on-site English lessons to businesspersons at various companies. If Rafael had a business lead, he'd telephone and offer immediate service. "This is Rafael from English Now! Would you like to begin conversation lessons tomorrow morning at seven?" Oftentimes, on short notice, our English teachers left their apartments at 5:30 a.m., lugging notebooks and student handouts through a series of city bus connections, in order to arrive at a company by seven o'clock. They'd teach an hour-long lesson, then navigate bus routes back to the school just in time to grab something to eat and take another set of buses to get to another company by noon. They'd repeat the process for their seven o'clock evening class.

Each week, teachers sat in front of my desk describing their frustrations. Crappy hours. Broken promises. Inadequate teaching materials. I met with Rafael. Told him that our teachers needed textbooks. "Textbooks aren't cheap, Laura," Rafael said.

I countered. "It's unreasonable to expect our teachers to supply their own teaching materials, Rafael."

Rafael smiled. "Yes, Laura. Our teachers need textbooks. That's why I placed a big order a few weeks ago." I checked with the school's secretary. Her records showed no textbook orders in the past four months. "I ordered loads of them!" Rafael insisted. Without blinking, he added, "The postal service is slow."

I talked with Rafael about the teachers' low morale. Their exhaustion. He threw me a bone. "I understand, Laura," he said. "Our teachers don't like their schedules. So, we'll change their schedules." An hour later, I heard him on the phone with a prospective client. "You'd like English lessons at eight o'clock on Tuesday and Thursday nights? No problem! You can start tomorrow."

At the end of one meeting, Rafael lamented that I wasn't as proficient in Spanish as he'd expected. "I was honest on my resume," I reminded him. "Spanish level: Lower intermediate. Remember?"

"Yes, I suppose." Rafael clicked his pen. "I just thought you'd be more, I don't know, fluent."

When it came to my Spanish ability, the Mexicans I chatted with were unfailingly polite. I'd strike up conversations at bus stops, in grocery stores. We'd chat about the weather, our jobs (*Soy maestra de idiomas,* I am a language teacher), our hobbies (*Me gusta cocinar,* I like to cook). Behind patient eyes, I'd catch momentary cringes when I said "mejor" (better) instead of "mayor" (older), "cochina" (filthy) instead of "cocina" (kitchen), "cabello" (hair) instead of "cebolla" (onion).

Rafael leaned back in his chair. "I knew someone who became fluent by watching Mexican movies with subtitles." He interlaced his fingers behind his head. "Try that."

"I'm trying to improve my Spanish," I told him. "But fluency doesn't happen overnight."

"Your Spanish doesn't need to be perfect, Laura. It just needs to be, I don't know, better."

When Cesar Millan crossed the border into the U.S., the first sentence in English he learned was, "Do you have application for work?" By the time he had his own television show, his English was very good, but not flawless. To me, his linguistic imperfections made him sound wise, prophetic. "Little thing create big problem," he'd say, as the camera zoomed in on a Chihuahua, the size of a kid's slipper, chewing apart a leather handbag. "Chihuahua, in his mind, is alligator."

I studied Rafael. His round, brown eyes. Thin, shaky hands. His propensity for snappishness. *Chihuahua, in his mind, is alligator.* My employment contract with English Now! promised twenty complimentary hours of Spanish classes. "You're right, Rafael. Time for my Spanish lessons," I said. "Can I get started this week?"

"Of course," Rafael said. "John mentioned wanting to take Spanish lessons. You two can take them together." John was a Canadian in his late twenties who'd been teaching at English Now! for nearly a year. "I'll call Ana Maria and confirm your class time."

Towering over six-foot-tall, John's thin body curved like a shepherd's crook as he slunk into my office. "Hey, John. Good news!" I said. John forced a grin, his dimples creased like coin slots. "Rafael said that you and I can start Spanish lessons this week."

John rubbed a hand over his blonde brush-cut and shot me a tired look. "Good luck with that," he said. "He's promised me free lessons since I arrived. Never happened."

"But he's confirmed with our teacher, Ana Maria," I told John. "This Thursday at 11:00 a.m." Then I added, "Bring a notebook."

"Sorry to burst your bubble," John said, "but I've seen how this movie ends."

Thursday morning at nine o'clock John and I received an email from Rafael explaining that Ana Maria had to cancel our lesson due to a sinus infection. "There's always something," John told me. "Death in the family, kids' babysitter crapped out on her, ear wax build-up, pubic lice, hemorrhoids…"

"Pubic lice? Really?"

"Yeah, and once she couldn't make it because she had a stye. A stye! Here Gus is legally blind and hauls his ass to work every day and Ana Maria cancels for a stye?"

Gus, an American teacher from North Dakota who'd worked at our school for over a year, saw objects at a distance mostly as shadows. He could determine optical details only when up-close and magnified. To read, Gus utilized special software and devices to enlarge digital and hard copy words and letters. He navigated sidewalks using a long, white cane that he tapped against curbs and cracks and potholes. Once, after a torrential downpour, Gus waded knee-deep through an intersection, tapping away at the water's crest. Fluent in Spanish and fiercely independent, I asked Gus how he managed to get around this traffic-intense city as a pedestrian and riding city buses. "It's a fucking pain in the ass," he said. That pretty much summed it up.

I jotted in my notebook, *Talk with Rafael about Spanish lessons!!!* "Sorry, John. I'll talk with Rafael again…"

"Pick your battles," John said, "It's more important that we get our work visas."

Most of our foreign teachers worked without visas. Every three months, Rafael asked them to re-send scans of their passports. Then he'd fill out a pile of paperwork, make some phone calls and put the teachers on an early bus to an American border city in hopes of obtaining visas. There was always some glitch. "Immigration has become impossible!" Rafael would say, slamming down the telephone receiver.

Rafael wrote our paychecks from his personal bank account. On pay days, I'd walk eight blocks to Rafael's bank to cash my check. "Por favor," I'd say sweetly to the bank teller. Rafael had discouraged me from trying to open a Mexican bank account on a tourist visa. I could feel my upper lip sweat as I asked to cash the check. The teller would narrow his eyes, summon the bank manager. The two would whisper – *This seems suspicious…a gringo cashing large personal checks every two weeks…* -- while punching keys on their computer.

"Un momento," the manager would say sternly. Eventually, "Tu pasaporte." Sliding my passport underneath the plexiglass window, I'd hold my breath until he shuffled back with an envelope full of pesos.

For months, Rafael had been stressed about our language school's upcoming inspection. English Now!, an international franchise, was sending a certified auditor from London. Three days before the inspector arrived, Rafael greeted me in our school's parking lot. "Here's the key!" he said, pointing to a pint-sized car he'd leased. It was a Chevy Sprint, I believe, or the Flintstone car that Barney Rubble once pedaled. The plan was that I'd chauffeur the visiting inspector around for a week, back and forth from his hotel to our school to client companies. Rafael patted the hood of the car. "It's primarily for business, but you can drive it home and use it to get around all you want."

For the past four years, I'd relied on public transportation. For the few months I'd lived in this heavily populated Mexican city, I walked or took the bus. I had limited geographical bearing. I had no GPS. Armed with my flip phone, rusty driving skills and directions scrawled on a legal pad, I'd merge in putt-putt mode onto the congested, frantic web of highways. I was terrified and looked the part – clutching the wheel with tensed shoulders, flicking my head to check for oncoming vehicles. I was suddenly one of those old ladies, the ones I'd formerly rolled my eyes at, who said things like, "I don't drive at night anymore. And in the rain? Forget it."

With a few days to practice before the inspector arrived, I drove to some of our client companies to meet with businesspersons or to drop off paperwork. I'd ask Rafael for directions. "It's easy," he'd say. "You just take Avenida Insurgentes Sur to Venustiano Carranza then turn left…no right, onto Calle El Risco, or maybe Calle Violetas, but soon you'll see a tall building and it'll be behind the building next to that…" I'd find myself going 50 miles per hour in my pony car, attempting to cross three lanes to make my exit, with trucks and buses whirring past me at 70 miles per hour. *Jesus! Drive much, lady? My grandmother drives faster than you!*

Our London-based inspector, Hugh, was in Mexico for two months, making rounds to English Now! schools across the country. Therefore, his most recent emails to me were about laundry. "Could you identify a launderette with twenty-four-hour turn around? My laundry needs are dire!"

On the afternoon of Hugh's arrival, I made the forty-minute drive, slow crawl, to the airport to pick him up. "It's nice to meet you," I said, extending my hand. "Good flight?"

"Long day," Hugh said, giving a quick sideways nod of his head to move us along. He was tall, jowly with tear-shaped nostrils the size of Gummy Sharks. "Launderette?" he asked. "You said you'd locate a launderette…"

I'd studied a precise route from the airport back to English Now! with a quick detour to drop paperwork off at Q&P Manufacturers, a company where we had clients enrolled in English lessons. "There's a launderette near our school," I said. "On our way, I need to make one quick stop at Q&P…"

"Actually," Hugh interrupted, "Could you drop me off at a café to grab a quick snack? Anywhere, really. A Starbucks, perhaps? You can pick me up after your errand." *You don't understand! I have directions – hand-written in very large letters -- for my exact route.* As we neared Q&P, Hugh pointed out the passenger's window. "We're in luck! Looks like a Starbucks off the next exit."

"I'll be back in a few minutes," I told Hugh as he stepped out of the car. Driving from Starbucks to Q&P was simple enough. I got back on the expressway and resumed my directions. After my errand at Q&P, I merged onto the expressway towards Starbucks. *Exit should be coming up soon…*

The exit I'd taken going north was not available southbound. *Stay calm.* I took the nearest exit. *You'll just have to back-track a bit.* I navigated a series of one-way streets, none of which circled back to Starbucks. *Shit! Okay, just get back on the expressway.* I was turned around. Wait a minute. I'm going north, right? Or should I now be going south? Is that the intersection I turned left on after I exited? *Oh my God, the inspector's probably wondering where the hell I am. Where the hell am I?* I pulled into a parking lot. Flipped open my phone. "Rafael!" I choked back tears. "I dropped the inspector off at Starbucks."

"Okay, that's fine. What time do you think you'll be here?"

"After I finished my errand, I went to pick him up and I…I can't find the road back to Starbucks…"

"You can't find Starbucks? It's the same one you dropped him off at."

"But on the highway, there wasn't an exit from the southbound lane, so I took the next exit…

"Laura," Rafael interjected, "Where are you now?"

"Uh, I'm on the corner of Avenida, uh, Presidente, I think…"

"Okay. Then how did you get there?"

"I got off the expressway and…took a right, no, a left and then went to the next intersection…Rafael, I'm LOST!"

"Laura, put your hands on the wheel and drive." Click.

Chihuahua, in his mind, is alligator.

I backtracked. Circled around. Finally landed on a side road that wove me near enough to Starbucks. I parked the car, ran across a greenway, through an automotive parts store parking lot and into Starbucks where the inspector sat at a square table, his thick grey eyebrows knitted in worry. I smiled, cleared my throat, and said brightly, "Ready to go to the school?"

Around that time, my face rash made its debut. Hot red, stress-induced bump clusters crowning in daily increments and, within a few weeks, snaking from the sides of my mouth and down my chin like an irate salamander. We'd passed our school inspection. The inspector was long gone, off to his next school with a carry-on full of clean socks and underwear. But my rash remained. We were in the midst of hiring season, filling English teacher vacancies. When Skype interviewing candidates, before pressing the online call button, I dimmed the office blinds and positioned myself an arm's length from the computer camera. Kept my rashy face at a distance.

"I see you have a bachelor's degree in English," I said to the interviewee, a young woman named Dottie from Winchester, England. She was twenty-five years old. Qualified. Poised. And so pleasant with her round-eyed, button face. "And a Cambridge teaching certificate, plus two years of classroom experience...Tell me, what interests you in this position?"

Dottie leaned toward the screen. "Well, I've always had a keen interest in teaching English in Central America, especially Mexico..." She talked about the excellent teaching evaluations she received from adult learners, her organized lesson planning system, her familiarity with speaking assessment tests. *Great! You're hired!* When I asked what questions she had for me, she tilted her chin up and said, "The employment ad says that free Spanish lessons are included. Will they begin right away?"

Before interviewing candidates, I met with Rafael to express my concerns about promising Spanish lessons and a speedy work visa when they hadn't materialized for our current teachers. "Rafael," I'd said, "I can't lie to prospective teachers."

"Laura, you won't need to lie to them," he'd responded. "But you don't need to tell them *everything.*" I sighed. He added, "When they ask about those things, just tell them those questions will be answered in *my* Skype interview with them."

"You'll tell them the truth about the work visa situation? And the Spanish lessons?"

"Of course," he'd said. It seemed that, when Rafael felt backed against a wall, his instinct was to bullshit his way out of the conflict. He was like the little, white dog named Cotton in the *Dog Whisperer* episode in which Cesar assessed the thirty-five-pound dog that snarled and gnashed its teeth toward Cesar's hands. "He has a weapon that is his mouth."

Rafael had shuffled papers on his desk and smiled. "I will tell the job candidates everything that they need to know." *He has a weapon that is his mouth.*

I looked through the screen at Dottie. At the way her nose turned up slightly when she smiled. "Ah, Spanish lessons....Um, that's a question for Rafael, the school proprietor," I told her. "You'll Skype with him later this week." My rash bumps crackled beneath my tawny-beige foundation.

In my first letter of resignation, I stated that I was leaving English Now! due to philosophical differences between myself and Rafael. "Philosophical differences!" Rafael yelled. "I can't tell Alonzo at Headquarters *that*!" I'm in an impossible situation, I told him. Working without a visa. Lying for him. Promising benefits to our teachers that I knew would not materialize. "Philosophical differences? You're the second Director of Studies who's quit in the last year. Alonzo will blow a fucking gasket!" We settled on a re-write. I was leaving Mexico and returning to the U.S. in order to be closer to my elderly parents who suffered from a variety of health problems. Arthritis, cardiac issues, respiratory challenges. My letter was half true.

Over the next two months, I applied for teaching jobs in the U.S. and accepted Skype interviews with a string of prospective employers. My rashy face positioned an arm's length from the computer camera lens, my office blinds pulled to half-mast.

PART III

MISGUIDED IN THE OZARKS

One thing that surprised me about dating in Fayetteville, Arkansas – a city of 85,000 residents nestled in the Ozark Mountains -- was that men oftentimes showed up for a first-time coffee date with a bouquet of flowers.

I hadn't set out to move to Arkansas. After casting a wide net in the job search arena, I'd received a few bites. I interviewed with the director of a language school in Los Angeles and another in Washington, D.C. But the conversations left me feeling disheartened. Long hours, low pay, high rent districts. When a school in Fayetteville requested an interview, I researched the area and grew enamored by Fayetteville's affordable cost of living, cultural proclivity, and natural beauty. I eagerly signed a teaching contract. Navigating Arkansas's geography was easy enough. Its dating landscape, however, felt like a whole new terrain.

In Rochester, I'd never received flowers when meeting a man for the first time in a cafe. There was the guy who brought me a pumpkin. Or was it a gourd. But flowers? Must be an Arkansas thing.

I was meeting Tom, a semi-retired businessman and photographer, who'd relocated to Arkansas from California a year or two before. According to his Match.com profile, Tom shared my philosophy when it came to assessing romantic connection. "Until you meet in person, you have no idea if there will be chemistry." He preferred arranging a quick and casual first meet. "I'm happy to meet someone in the Walmart bread aisle," he'd written. "If there's attraction, we can arrange a date. If not, we're off to price check cheese." *Amen to that, brother.* Nearly a decade before, when I'd first started dating after my divorce, I agreed to dinner at an Italian restaurant with a man I hadn't even talked with over the phone. Email courtship. Before our dinner date, I'd shaved my toes, put on sandals and a skirt. The man had put on a tie and doused himself in Old Spice. For two hours of slow service, we forced polite conversation. *Jeez, how long does it take to boil spaghetti?* In the parking lot, we air hugged. Falsely claimed, "That was fun!" Then fled to our cars.

Lesson learned. I generally knew within five minutes of meeting in person whether or not there was a connection. Make first-meets brief.

I emailed Tom. Suggested meeting at Ozark Natural Foods in the frozen edamame aisle. Tom responded quickly. He'd enjoyed reading my profile, he said. "Actually," he wrote. "You lived in Asia and I've been there too. Why not meet for a quick glass of wine at the Mill House? Compare travel notes?"

Why not.

The Mill House hostess tapped a pen against the seating chart. "I'm meeting someone here," I said. She fingered her earring and stifled a yawn. "A gentleman named Tom…"

The hostess glanced up; her pupils dilated. "Right this way!" We turned the corner and I saw him. Silver-haired handsome. Seated at a round table for six. The tabletop was covered with a *This Is My Life* display which included his jumbo-lensed camera, favorite books, photo albums and a bouquet of flowers, the size I'd seen Olympic ice skaters haul off rinks. *Whatever happened to a quick hello in the bread aisle?*

Tom stood, grasped my hands in his. Cold fingers. "I've looked forward to meeting you," he said. His eyes were more gray than blue, like buttons on a cadet coat. "I'd love to hear about your travels." I clicked my teeth together in a tight smile, studying the tabletop display. "As you can see, I brought a few things to help you get to know me, but first," he said, lifting the voluminous flower bouquet with both hands, "for you!"

A waiter walked past. Grinned, winked. A woman on her way to the restroom gave me a thumbs up. Sweat pooled in the small of my back. My face flushed beet. Tom poured two glasses of Cabernet. "Cheers," he said, lifting his glass, "to the adventurer!" Then he was on a roll – showing me photographs he'd published professionally, flipping through photos of himself, smiling and sun-kissed, stretched out on a yacht, sitting in a Mercedes. He'd been fortunate, he said. Good education, generous parents, successful in business. He mentioned that he loved my profile photos – the one of me feeding an elephant in Thailand and holding babies in Ethiopia.

I tried many times to interject. Leaned forward, opened my mouth to squeak out a word or two. Tom seemed oblivious. His voice rumbled on. A never-ending freight train. Would that train ever take a detour? Better yet, crash and burn? A wave of guilt washed through me. *He brought you flowers, took the time to truck all his life crap to the table. For you!* But as he rambled on, the guilt was overtaken by annoyance. "I've been divorced for a while now," Tom said. He'd been married for twenty-five years to a woman from Vietnam. "She didn't know a word of

English when I met her." He swirled the wine in his glass. "Didn't matter to me. In fact, it was great..."

I glanced at my watch. "I teach an early class tomorrow, need to prepare…"

Tom raised his hand to usher the waiter. "The veal marsala here is exquisite," he said. "And they have a nice crab and prawn bisque…"

"Sounds lovely, but I really do need to…"

"Nonsense," he said, then lifted his chin toward the waiter. "We'll start with the pistachio crusted goat cheese."

Nonsense? He'd dismissed me. My annoyance turned to anger, and I rummaged through my purse for car keys. "Thank you for the wine and flowers, Tom…"

"Seriously?" His thin undereye skin puffed beneath narrowed eyes.

"Yes. It was nice meeting you…"

Tom leaned toward me. "You know, I don't think you're an adventurer at all," he said, folding his arms on the tabletop. "Four years of moving from country to country. You're just LOST!"

For a guy who'd spent the last forty-minutes talking rather than listening -- informing me about the details of his life rather than inquiring about mine – I had to admit, he was on to something.

After spending nearly four years living overseas, relocating from South Korea to South America, from Spain to Mexico then returning "home" to the United States, but to Arkansas, a state I hadn't even driven through before, I did feel rather lost. Was it really that obvious?

Out of Step

In Fayetteville, I taught English at the Language Institute of Arkansas, a school for adult international students. In the school's cafeteria, my fellow ESL instructor, Jerry, propped a forearm on the Formica tabletop. "Let's talk grammar!" he said. "Absolute phrases, for starters." His blue eyes lit elfin-like. "I'm on track to cover absolute phrases in my Monday/Wednesday class this week." He gave a fresh-faced, can-do smile. "What are some of your favorite lesson activities?" Fortunately, another colleague, Lisa, sat at the table with us, eating lunch and pumping out conversational tidbits, so the question wasn't directed at me individually.

Lisa piped up, "I have my students write phrases containing a noun plus linking verb plus past participle plus prepositional phrase."

Jerry's wispy brows furrowed on his freckled forehead. "How about absolutes with a noun plus adjective, noun plus past participle?"

Lisa shot Jerry a quizzical glance. "Well, that just goes without saying."

Jesus Christ. On what planet does this pass for lunch conversation? I'd experienced a similar out-of-universe sensation at our last teachers' meeting during which my fellow educators slung around terminology -- capstone project, impactful practice, plurilingualism, communicative language competences -- the way a baby baboon flings its own poop.

In that meeting, Brenda had asserted, "Our main focus should be a curriculum that echoes a learner-centered approach..."

I'd jotted the word "learner" in my notebook, updating my list of that week's academically correct jargon. Apparently, "student" was out, and "learner" was in. Earlier, I'd received the stink eye from colleagues when referring to individual students as "you know, the skinny one with the frizzy hair who burps a lot" and "the older one who wears squeaky corduroy." With a red pen, I underlined "learner" for emphasis.

At the meeting, Sam had cut in, "I'd like to piggyback on what Brenda said. Curriculum must be both learner-centered and applicable…"

"I'm going to dovetail on Sam's comment," Justin had interjected. "In a learner-centered approach, the application…"

Piggyback on what Brenda said. Dovetail on Sam's comment. I wanted a custom-printed coffee mug -- Get off my piggyback!

In the cafeteria, Lisa set her tuna sandwich on her napkin and asked, "Do any of you have examples of predicate pronouns that students can relate to?" *Oh, God.* I spooned Grape Nuts into my yogurt. *Please don't look at me. Please don't ask me. Please let Jerry answer.*

Jerry cleared his throat. "That's an easy one," he said. "It was *he* who rapped at the Grammy awards." I'd seen Jerry in the teacher's lounge twenty minutes earlier showing a co-worker his PowerPoint slide on semi-colons. "*He* is obviously the predicate pronoun because it completes the meaning of the linking verb *was* and refers to the subject *It.*"

I stirred my cereal into a yogurt swirl. *No one likes a grammarian. If someone had to choose between dining at a restaurant straight from work with a septic tank cleaner, sea lion feeder or grammarian, the grammarian would lose every time.*

"Thanks, Jerry," Lisa said. "That example is so *relatable.* You know, with the word *rap* and all." Lisa typed the sentence into her cell phone Notes and added, "I was using the example *The principal of the school was she*, but yours is much hipper."

I was sitting at a cafeteria table feeling outsmarted by a couple of know-it-alls. The experience felt like my childhood all over again. Jerry and Lisa were probably the kids who played teacher for fun. Rounding up younger neighborhood kids and tormenting them for hours with classroom ground rules and handwriting a flawless cursive "G." Most likely, they were the high schoolers who volunteered as teacher shadows and after-school writing tutors.

I, on the other hand, was always a step behind.

*

While my older siblings were away at college meeting stringent scholastic requirements and excelling in honors courses, I played the cymbals in my high school marching band. The cymbals were not my instrument of choice. Our band's best percussionists, the ones capable of aptly drumming double stroke rolls, single paradiddles and flam-taps, played the snares. The big-boned kid with strong arms and a decent sense of rhythm, played bass drum. The drummer who was good at reading music notes, was assigned the xylophone. Percussionists like me, who wanted to play the drums without actually practicing the drums, were left with either the triangle, cowbell or cymbals. I drew the short straw.

On summer parade days, we marched down flag-decorated Main Streets in muggy July heat, my sweaty palms gripping the looped straps of my cymbals – a pair of pewter circles the size of manhole covers. We band members played on, while keeping step over potholes and steaming mounds of parade-horse shit.

Our band uniforms were stiff and heavy. A flat-collared blazer with corded shoulders. Navy blue pants. White spats. A box hat with plume. The kind you might find on a disgruntled circus bear.

A few hours before parade time, uniforms were doled out in the music room by Mrs. Combs, the band leader's mother. Her eyebrows were penciled in tawny brown. Her yellow hair was teased into a knoll atop her head. When I stepped up to the uniform rack, she checked the size box on her inventory sheet and said, "Husky."

Most of us huskies sweat a lot while marching. Husky uniforms smelled like spoiled cottage cheese. My blazer fit fine, but the crotch of the snug nylon slacks tugged unevenly. I always seemed to get the hat plume, which resembled a white feather duster, with the half-broken stem. My plume teetered to the left while I marched, giving the impression that, if I weren't boxed between the snare drum cadet and xylophone player, I'd march in counterclockwise circles. Like a mad clown car.

I clanked my cymbals to *We are the Champions.* Marched to *Play that Funky Music.* I was a high school senior, a solid "B" student, who hadn't gotten around to applying to any universities. Most of the other girls in my graduating class seemed to have a planned trajectory. Many would head off to private or state universities. Others had enrolled in community college classes for fall semester. Some would train to become dental hygienists or cosmetologists. I could see only as far ahead as the wrapped Tootsie Rolls and Life Savers the parade master had tossed onto the pavement for spectators to scavenge. I marched in place, tapping my cymbals to *Spinning Wheel.* With each rhythmic step, my husky-girl parade slacks sawed further into the crack of my ass.

One day, I discovered an advertisement on the back page of a magazine. Wilma Boyd Travel School. At the bottom of the ad was an 800 number. I dialed it. "Uh, hi," I said. "I saw your ad about travel school?" The woman on the other end would be delighted, she said, to detail the "thrilling travel opportunities" available for Wilma Boyd graduates. We scheduled a home visit.

The travel school recruiter arrived at our house on a Saturday morning. "Greetings! I'm Katherine," she announced, placing her briefcase, gorged with brochures and paperwork, at the head of our kitchen table. Katherine wore barn red lipstick. Her honey beige foundation ended abruptly at her fleshy jawline.

"Lovely home," Katherine said, glancing at our Kmart window valances and the kitty litter box in the corner of the room. Katherine drew in a sharp breath. The buttons of her polyester dress strained against her gut as if about to burst from her enthusiasm. "I'm here to get you started on your exciting life in travel!"

Katherine took a seat, her torso blubber bubbling above the waistline of her girdle. "After completing the three-month course of study at Wilma Boyd Travel School," she began, "our graduates have been hired at Trans World Airways, Carnival

Cruise Lines, and both corporate and leisure travel agencies around the country." Pulling a glossy brochure from her arsenal of sales supplies, Katherine continued, "And that's because the Wilma Boyd curriculum is highly-respected among travel industry representatives."

My pulse quickened. *Airlines! Cruise lines! Corporate travel agencies!* I nodded in awe. Katherine went in for the big sell. Sliding her chair from beneath the table, she pivoted toward me. "Now, Laurie, this well-regarded program is rigorous," she cautioned. "I'm not saying it's going to be easy." She drove a focused gaze through her clumped mascara. "But I can tell you're the kind of studious young woman who can be successful." From her faux-pearl earrings to the pantyhose that bunched at her ankles, this woman, to me, was success personified. And *she* had confidence in *my* abilities. "Now, Laurie, are you ready to get paid to travel the world?"

I was.

I scrolled my full name on the bottom line of the travel school application. Signed a student loan agreement – my cross-your-heart-not-your-fingers promise to fork over two thousand dollars in easy installments of seventy-nine bucks per month. I envisioned working as part of a close-knit flight crew. Instructing passengers to buckle their seatbelts low and tight. Reminding them, in the case of emergency, to ignore their pesky lap child gasping for air and place an oxygen mask on their own faces first. I'd stride down aircraft aisles, in my svelte-size straight skirt and two-button blazer. Roll the beverage cart while gently cautioning, "Elbows and knees. Kindly watch your elbows and knees."

Two days after high school graduation, I headed off to Wilma Boyd Travel School near the booming metropolis of Pittsburgh, Pennsylvania. Before Wilma Boyd founded her travel institute, she taught at a small charm school. That explained why, along with classes in cruise ship safety regulations and airline tariffs, we Wilmas participated in a Dress for Success class taught by a former runway model.

In Dress for Success, the former model – a bony blonde in her fifties – showed us how to match the right neck scarf with the right A-line skirt. She also talked about the importance of a good skin care regime. "We all get a blemish from time to time," she confided. "My advice is, 'Leave it!'" She said this the way an impatient Cocker Spaniel owner commands, "Leave it!" when the dog sticks its snout into a dead bird's tailfeathers or licks up a dollop of goose poop. "You start your morning with a little pink dot on your face," the model continued, wagging a finger. "But instead of covering it with the right shade of concealer, you start picking." She raised her sparse eyebrows. "And the next thing you know, that little dot becomes a big, red pizza." Since my Wilma Boyd recruiter, Katherine, had considered me a studious young woman fully capable of academic rigor, I opened my notebook and jotted, *Don't pick zits.* This appeared on the same page I'd written, *New York LaGuardia Airport = LGA, 35 minutes minimum flight connection,* and *cafeteria guy looks like good kisser.*

At Wilma Boyd commencement – after spending three months of our lives studying airport abbreviation codes, designing travel itineraries, and memorizing airline layover time allowances -- our graduating class tossed around affirmations like, "I know you'll be successful" and "You're going to go far."

At the age of eighteen, I pounded the pavement. With my resume and Wilma Boyd graduation certificate in hand, I walked through the doors of travel agencies and asked my rehearsed question – "Is your supervisor, by any chance, available to meet with a certified travel agent in search of employment?" Since entry level travel agent wages were typically low, the turnover rate of such agents tended to be high. Three weeks into job hunting, I received a phone call from the manager of Time-to-Travel. They had an unanticipated opening. How soon could I start?

At nine o'clock the following morning I sat at a desk, staring at a wall-rack of travel brochures and spinning a globe. At Time-to-Travel, I booked honeymoon packages for couples with pre-wedding jitters and business flights for men in wrinkled shirts and clasped ties. I helped other people go far.

Between my studio apartment rent and monthly seventy-nine-dollar student loan payment, I had just enough money left over from my paycheck to sustain myself on white rice sprinkled with processed parmesan cheese.

In hopes of, someday, increasing my earning potential, I continued my day job at the travel agency and registered for evening classes at a local community college -- English Composition, Life Drawing I, and Introduction to Sociology.

One afternoon, while on my lunch break at Time-to-Travel, the agency owner entered our employee lounge. While microwaving a Sesame Chicken Lean Cuisine, she gave me the once over in my capris and short-sleeved blouse. "Here at Time-to-Travel," she said, "we like our team to dress like professionals." *Hmm...buying new clothes. For dinner this month, do I give up the rice or the Kraft Parmesan Cheese?* During my lunch break, I did homework. That day, I was finishing a sketch for my Drawing the Human Body assignment – applying pit and groin shadows with a 5B charcoal pencil.

Soon after, a thirty-five-year-old mother of two school-aged children was brought onboard as a Time-to-Travel intern. She was keen on learning the travel business. The woman entered the agency each morning wearing just the right neck scarf with her A-line skirt.

Since Time-to-Travel was all about opportunities, that intern was given the opportunity to work as a full-time travel agent. And I was given the opportunity to devote myself full-time to college. "Oh, uh, thank you," I'd initially said, when the agency owner detailed my "opportunity" one Friday afternoon. "You can start studying full-time on Monday," she said, then added, "at your college, I mean. Not here."

It stunk being fired, but I suppose it was for the best. The experience nudged me into exploring options I may not have otherwise considered. My first priority was a paycheck. I signed up with a Temp service and secured a steady stream of short-term reception and secretarial jobs. By day, I answered telephones, typed memos, filed paperwork, made coffee. At night, I sat in front of the TV conjuring ways to scrounge up money for college. One evening, a television commercial caught my attention. "Be all that you can be..." a background chorus sang as athletic young men wearing military camouflage proudly parachuted out of a perfectly good airplane. "…in the Army." *Be all that you can be.* I was a twenty-year-old office worker with chin acne earning twenty-five cents above minimum wage. I had the nagging suspicion that I needed to be more than I was.

The next day, during my lunch hour, I met with a recruiter wearing creased Army green slacks. He talked about military pay, benefits, patriotism then asked, "You're a high school graduate, right? Not GED?" When I nodded, he thumbed through a spreadsheet and said, "There are openings for cooks, truck drivers and field radio repairers." Straightening the pressed sleeves of his blazer, he added, "Choose one and sign here."

I left the recruiting center with a four-year contract to serve in the Army Reserves where I'd receive training to, first, be a soldier and, second, a field radio repairer. I didn't know what exactly was involved in repairing field radios, but I knew it sounded cooler than changing oil in a military utility vehicle or boiling and mashing thirty-five pounds of potatoes every day. Within a month, I headed off to nine weeks of Boot Camp in Fort Jackson, South Carolina, where I learned how to properly clear and seal a protective gas mask, bayonet-stab obstacle course dummies, and low crawl under barbed wire in combat gear and night vision goggles. Since the Army confiscated my civilian belongings -- including tweezers – I also learned how to grow a unibrow the length of a baby weasel.

After nearly a year of active-duty training, I returned to Rochester where I carried out weekend duty as an Army Reservist. With financial support from the new G.I. Bill and a low interest student loan, I crammed my schedule with college courses. Four years later, I attended a graduation where people asked, "A degree in *English*? What the hell are you planning to do with *that*?"

*

One of the classes I taught at the English Language Institute of Arkansas was Level Basic Writing and Grammar. When it came to learner level hierarchy, you couldn't go lower than Level Basic. It was the midget on the height comparison graph, the Pre-Cambrian bedrock of the sedimentary strata.

Level Basic was, I ascertained, the level for romantics – for expats who, rather than studying the language intensely before leaving their home country, simply wiped away any nagging concerns and decided, "I'll just pick up English when I get there!" Many arrived in the U.S. with two overstuffed suitcases, a college degree from their homeland, and the ability to count in English from one to twenty and recall a random animal word like *tapir* or *bobcat* only to be faced with the humiliation of earning a grade of 72 on my *What day is it?* quiz.

My classroom was spacious and square with a wall of windows overlooking a wide strip of grass on which, after a good rain, two or three ducks, squat and heavy-bottomed, ambled along. I set my books and folders on the front desk and distributed Dry Erase markers in a variety of colors on the aluminum lower lip of the whiteboard. With a purple marker, I wrote *past tense* to refresh my students' memories of last week's lesson.

"Good morning!" I said. Lanying and Noura forced anxious grins in my direction then studied their desktops. They knew what was coming – a Monday morning question/answer session. Surveying the room, I asked, "How *was* your weekend?" Falad stared at the whiteboard. *Don't call on me, don't call on me, please, dear God, don't call on me…*

Turning toward Xiaobo, a lanky young man with black hair gel-sculpted into a crest, I asked, "Xiaobo? Your weekend?" He bit the corner of his lip. "How *was* it? What *did* you do?"

Xiaobo ran the back of his slender hand along his chin. "Oh, so nervous."

"No nervous," I consoled. Sometimes to get my message across efficiently, I spoke to my students in what I called "chicken talk," by simply cheeping out key words rather than bantering about in fluid, snakelike sentences. I could have said, "Oh, there's no need for you to be nervous, Xiaobo. Just tell me about your weekend using verbs in past tense." But then I'd be left to watch sweat bubbles multiply on poor Xiaobo's upper lip as he mentally sifted through my sentences before finally picking out the words that mattered: *no, nervous, tell, weekend.*

"I study," Xiaobo answered. Then added in a stilted voice, "I study English."

"Very good!" I said. He may not have answered using past tense, but he produced three English words in a logical sequence and, besides, he had cool hair.

"Okay." I underlined the words *past tense* written on the board. "A few more questions..." I stood beside Falad. "In Saudi Arabia, what *did* you do for work?" I asked.

Falad ran a hand through his black wavy hair. "Uh, I am teach for math."

"And *before* that?" I asked. "What *did* you do?"

"Uh, before, I am student."

"Very good!" I said. His answers were, after all, consistent. And, besides, who was I to crap on his Monday by being critical? I'd never be nominated for Educator of the Year, but at least I could be nice.

As I moved toward Lanying's desk, I mentally noted that present tense was clearly my students' tense of preference. And I did want to create a learner-centered environment, didn't I? "Lanying," I began, "in China, what does your father do?"

"Mmm..." Lanying picked at her thumbnail. "Father dead."

"Oh, so sorry," I said.

Lanying nodded. "Father do dead."

"Okay, let's turn to our homework," I suggested before Lanying's dead father stewed everyone into a Monday morning funk. "Page thirty-six. Yes/No questions. Questions that can be answered with a 'yes' or a 'no.'"

I shot a smile at Majed who sat slumped at his desk wearing a black hoodie pulled tight. In red marker, I wrote on the board, *Is Majed singing?*

"Is Majed singing?" I asked at the volume of a blaring radio. The students turned to look at Majed who sat close-mouthed with an expression that seemed to be asking *What?* "Class," I said. "Is Majed singing?"

Silence. Reaching my hand to the small of my back, I tugged at my sweaty blouse. "Anyone? Is Majed singing?"

Alaweed shifted in his seat then offered, "Yes, Majed swimming, I think."

"Thank you, Alaweed! Good!" I exclaimed because in my class talking nonsense was better than not talking at all.

Am I dancing? I wrote on the board. "Am I dancing, Haneul?" I asked, standing stiffly in front of the whiteboard with my hands clasped.

"Yes," Haneul mumbled while shaking her head.

"Dancing?" I pressed, standing wooden and motionless. "Am I dancing?"

Haneul gazed at the whiteboard, mouthing, "yes."

"Well, uh," I began. "No. I'm not dancing." Appearing disheartened, Haneul turned her gaze to the floor. "Well, I'm not dancing *right now*, but I may dance *later,"* I said then leaned toward Haneul. "So, Yes! I will be dancing." Haneul's dark eyes brightened before a look of utter confusion crossed her delicate face.

Am I a shitty teacher? I imagined writing on the board as a room full of students shouted in chorus, "Yes!"

"One more question," I said, sweating like a fifth grader in a spelling bee assigned the word *conjunctivitis*.

In blue marker I wrote *Am I marching?* Lifting my knees high and pumping my arms, I marched across the front of the room.

"Mingshu. Am I marching?" Mingshu peeked over at Xiaobo. "Am I marching, Mingshu?" I asked, marching like a parade master from one end of the room to the other.

"Yes," Mingshu said.

"Very good!" I said, feeling spent and victorious.

Mingshu beamed then added, "Majed is sing, I think."

One Plus One

Bruce, a sixty-one-year-old mathematician, who lived in a college town in Oklahoma, 175 miles west of my place in Fayetteville, sent me an email. Match.com again. He'd read my online dating profile and liked the story I'd written about two dogs I'd cared for, Blanca and Guapo, who shared a kennel at the animal shelter in Peru. The canines were loving, playful, loyal companions. I was looking, I'd written, for my Guapo.

Bruce introduced himself. Told me, briefly, about his work as a college administrator who continued to teach a math course every semester. Described his quiet life in Stillwater. I clicked on his featured profile photo -- a close-up of him sitting at his desk. His wavy hair and beard were dark brown with hints of gray. His hazel eyes looked kind.

I eagerly read Bruce's bio. He was divorced. Liked birdwatching. Grew up Quaker. He'd checked the box that said he owned a dog. A Border Collie, Blue Heeler mix. Then added a note. *Truth be told, my dog, Skye, died recently.* He hadn't had the heart to leave the box unchecked.

I wrote him back immediately and a dialogue began. Soon, Bruce noted that we seemed to have a fair amount in common. We both enjoyed teaching. Liked to travel. Had big hearts for animals. He asked, "Would it be too pushy of me to ask for your phone number?"

It wasn't.

I sent him my cell and Bruce called right away. His voice sounded warm, his laughter sincere. I learned that he enjoyed yard work and gardening, that his Turk's caps had bloomed beautifully last summer. He learned that I was a fan of yoga and walking and that I'd competed in a few marathons and was quite sure I'd taken the title of slowest runner ever. We talked a bit about work and the weather, the varied landscapes of Oklahoma and Arkansas. Then Bruce burst out, "Could I take you to lunch in Fayetteville this Sunday afternoon?"

I froze. This would be our first in-person meeting. A quick coffee was my mode of operation. "We could meet halfway," I suggested. "How about coffee in Tulsa?"

Bruce knew the geography better than I and pointed out that Tulsa wasn't really halfway; I'd be driving two hours to his one. "I enjoy driving," Bruce assured me. "And it's April, a beautiful time of year." We were silent for a moment, then Bruce said, "Fayetteville, please?"

I bit my lip then cleared my throat. "I'll make reservations."

Two days before our lunch date, my nerves kicked in. Bruce was driving 175 miles to meet me for lunch. At some point during our correspondence, I'd wondered aloud why my Match.com profile had come up on his search, but his profile hadn't come up on mine. "Probably has to do with your online dating range," he'd said. That's right. Mine was set at one hundred miles. Bruce had opened his search to a 300-mile radius. At the time, I hadn't thought much of that tidbit of information. But now that I'd agreed to defy my rule -- make first-meets brief -- and Bruce was driving three hours to take me to lunch, my stomach roiled with uncertainty. Was he desperate?

I opened my laptop and studied Bruce's posted photographs. There was one of him taken at a funny angle, standing in front of a closet door in which he looked short. Diminutive, even. His profile stated that he was five-foot seven. Was he really four-foot ten? He was driving all that way. Maybe with blocks on gas pedal and brake.

My gaze circled back to the headshot of Bruce in which his eyes appeared kind, his bearded face gentle, his lips soft. Our phone conversation was nice, I reminded myself. Really very nice. Then I went to the mall and bought a new blouse -- a tealy-mint green to wear with jeans and sandals. I did sit-ups. Polished my toenails. More sit-ups.

The morning of our lunch date, I had anxiety diarrhea. Skipped coffee, ate dry toast. Fifteen minutes before noon, I unlocked my car, the used Toyota Corolla I'd bought when I first arrived in Fayetteville. Its blue paint peeled in patches and the hood was covered in a film of pollen, but there was no time to make it more presentable now. I slid into the driver's seat, tilted the visor and applied a slick layer of tinted Chapstick – Sunset Nude. By the time I turned off Joyce Boulevard and onto Crossover Road, my hands had stopped shaking and my stomach fluttered with anticipation rather than anxiety.

When I pulled into the restaurant parking lot, I recognized Bruce immediately. Stocky, bearded, dark wavy hair. He was pacing back and forth in front of Apple Blossoms Brewing Company. I sighed relief. He was five-foot seven. I parked in back, checked my lip gloss again. I'd brought Bruce a bottle of wine in a gift bag. A consolation gift in case things didn't work out after he'd put in all that mileage. I walked to the front of the restaurant then toward Bruce who stood empty handed. No flowers. No pumpkin. He looked at me and smiled. "It's you," he said, rushing toward me with his palms facing skyward. "It's you!" he repeated as if we'd met in a previous life. I quickened my gait. His hands were so warm.

*

After that day, Bruce and I were together most weekends. On Fridays, I'd make the three-hour drive to Stillwater, or he'd drive to Fayetteville. The following forty-eight hours would rush by in a blur of passion, our bodies and minds ravenous for connection.

On Monday mornings, my colleagues would study me and grin. "There's something different about you," they'd say. And I'd wonder, can they smell it on me? The sex?

On weekdays, Bruce and I would chat on the phone while I walked park paths and Bruce chopped vegetables for dinner. Other times, we talked before bedtime, long calls about nothing important. We'd dial one another and fall into fluid conversations without beginnings or ends that felt like a warm, fuzzy bathrobe around my shoulders, like a lullaby.

With time and familiarity, a sense of playfulness emerged and when I answered the phone, Bruce would ask, "Is this Cakes? Miss Baby Cakes?"

I'd chuckle and think, God, he's such a mush. Then, holding the phone to my ear, I'd say, "Yes, this is she."

Sometimes Bruce and I would toss our heads back or clutch our stomachs laughing over how much we adored one another's bodies. These fifty- and sixty-year-old legs and bellies and saggy asses of ours that drove one another crazy with desire.

Other times we'd walk hand in hand in silence, glancing at one another quizzically. Hmm. There's something between us, isn't there? Something that makes our knees weak, stomachs flutter, hearts clamor.

One evening, a few months into our relationship, I lounged on Bruce's sofa -- in pajama pants and oversized T-shirt, my hair pulled into a high pony – studying my man. Bruce was wearing an ankle-length longyi that he'd bought years before during a trip to Bangladesh. I watched him standing at the kitchen counter scooping ice cream into bowls. Bare chested in his longyi, the fabric knotted at his waist. And I thought, who is this bearded Quaker man in slippers and a skirt? Then smiled with the realization, "It's him."

On sunny afternoons Bruce would suggest going to Boomer Lake and we'd walk the nearly treeless path around the manmade body of water. By halfway around, Bruce would be limping. That arthritic right knee of his. Bone scraping bone. We'd stop to watch great blue heron, their grey torso feathers puffed and shagged like an old lady's matted fur wrap. I'd take in my surroundings – the flat land and expanse of prairie grass, such a profoundly different landscape from my former home in the northeast. "God, I miss trees and rolling hills," I'd tell Bruce. Then kiss his neck and add, "But I've never seen such wide-open sky."

Sometimes Bruce baffled me by referring to himself by the pronoun *one.* He'd say, "One doesn't necessarily understand all manner of things."

I thought it was an old-time Quaker thing. "You mean, *you* don't understand," I'd ask.

Bruce was a mathematician, but his favorite thing was words. One evening as we sat on my small apartment balcony drinking Pinot Grigio and eating Hummus with celery sticks, I said, "Rather than a numbers person, you seem more like a Linguistics kind of guy."

Bruce responded, "The statement of a theorem requires precise language." Then he talked about the extent to which math required commitment. "One could work for years trying to prove a theorem," he said. "Then discover that it's not even true." Starting in graduate school, Bruce had worked on a theorem for eight years with no luck. "Then some Brainiac solved it."

"Jeez, after all that work," I said. "I mean, how'd you feel about that?"

"One can't resent such things," Bruce said. "It's the nature of mathematics."

"Yeah, but can't *you* resent it?"

Bruce shrugged. "The other mathematician was able to do the work when I wasn't." Then he confessed, "Actually, it did really piss me off."

That Monday morning, my colleagues ran their eyes the length of my body and smiled. "You look great!" they told me. Could they see it on me? The happiness?

I was happy. I was falling in love with a wonderful man who was murmuring words of love and commitment. But mostly, I was scared shitless. Bruce's constitution seemed one of steadfastness; his life appeared to be the definition of "settled." After four years of traveling the world on my own, I felt fiercely independent and filled with uncertainty about which direction to turn. Continuing in the direction of autonomy seemed to offer freedom, but with that the risk of losing Bruce. Taking a detour toward commitment seemed to offer assurance and security, but with that came an obligation that felt constraining. In the end, I followed my instinct to stay in motion, to head toward new places, to peruse the possibilities.

I'd chosen carefully what to wear for my Skype interview with the hiring committee at University of Toledo, but the camera angle made me visible from only the shoulders up. I sat at my desk in pressed blue slacks, black pumps, and a starched white shirt, facing a group of faculty members who were cordial and earnest and asked challenging questions. At the end of the interview, I thanked them, not certain at all about whether they were still considering me for the position or had crossed me off their list.

A few weeks later, at 7:30 a.m. as I was heading out the door to go to work, I received a phone call from a faculty member in the Department of English. I'd gotten the job. During fall semesters, I'd teach English Composition to international students on campus at the University of Toledo. Spring semesters I'd teach a Chinese cohort at their sister university in Hangzhou. This university Lecturer position was a step up from my current job as instructor at a language school. In Toledo, I'd reap the benefits of teaching on a college campus. Then have the opportunity to explore parts of China while teaching in Hangzhou. Initially, I was elated. Then heartbroken at the thought of leaving Bruce.

That evening, I called Bruce.

Exhaling a shaky breath, I said, "We need to talk."

"Hmm. That doesn't sound good."

I blurted, "I was offered a better job. A much better job. More money. A renewable contract…"

"Okay," Bruce said. "I was bracing myself for *We're better off as friends.*"

"It's in Toledo," I added. "Starting in August."

"Oh, uh, alright." He sighed. "Toledo."

"Well, I'll teach in Toledo during fall semester, but in spring semester, starting in February…"

"I'm listening."

"I'll teach in Hangzhou."

"Hangzhou?"

"Yes. Hangzhou, China."

There was a long silence on Bruce's end. I swallowed hard, trying to brace myself for an abrupt end to our conversation, to our relationship. Then Bruce cleared his throat. "Well, you know, Cakes…"

"Yes?"

"There's this wonderful invention. It's called the airplane."

WAITING TO FLY

At the age of fifty-three, I rented a room in student housing, a short walk to the academic building where I taught classes at the University of Toledo. Like others in student housing, I had a mini-fridge, microwave, and a thin foam mattress with vinyl cover. When I wasn't teaching, I holed up in my office or the library and took long walks while talking to Bruce.

There was a city park that I loved, an easy half-mile walk from my room. I'd jog the park trails then sit on a bench and breathe in the woodsy landscape that reminded me of home in upstate New York.

Oftentimes, in a Black Walnut tree near that bench I'd watch a number of crows, maybe ten or a dozen, making a ruckus. They'd caw, click their beaks as I marveled over those highly intelligent birds that congregated in groups. A murder of crows, it's called, which I learned was aptly named. If a crow in their group was harmed, its brethren crows would identify, track down and mob the perpetrator. Crows, I discovered, never forgot a face. I'd watch them gather on high branches, convene their flock meeting, then, in a flurry, fly into blue sky.

Halfway through my teaching semester, prompted by an interest in community service, I taught a creative writing workshop at a men's maximum-security prison. Colleagues who'd taught at the prison explained that to afford these men dignity, I should refer to them as "incarcerated individuals." This as opposed to "prisoners" or "inmates" or the more antiquated "jailbirds." I'd hear myself say, "Ten *incarcerated individuals* signed up for my writing workshop," secretly believing that the road to dignity would more likely start with the inmates' ability to, say, walk to the prison van shackle-free or choose to wear something besides oversized pants in America's Brightest Orange.

There's mostly gray in prison – pale, stone-gray walls, dark pewter lightbulb cages, steel-gray officer uniforms. All of the men in my workshop were Black. The eleven of us, myself and the ten men, congregated in a tight classroom on the prison's second floor, which was furnished with a square conference table that could squeeze twelve along with a small, corner desk, the size you might find in a community college study room.

I split our ninety-minute class period in two. In the first half, we read and analyzed essays and book excerpts by published authors. During the second half, I prompted creative writing exercises and we listened and responded to work written by the incarcerated individuals. Unlike my undergraduate students at the university, these men were diligent in completing homework assignments. Read and be prepared to talk about Chapter one of Richard Wright's *Black Boy.* No problem. They entered the prison classroom with margin-notated handouts, ready to discuss.

The prison buzzer sounded and the ten men streamed from the corridor into our classroom. Coleman, a sturdily built gentleman in his forties, I'd guess, slid an unoccupied chair from beneath the conference table. "Here, Woodford," he said, gesturing for me to take a seat.

In this penitentiary classroom, there was no such thing as being on a first name basis. I learned this from Jan, the middle-aged administrative clerk who accompanied me during the workshop. "We don't address each other by first names here," she said. Jan explained the rules in a pleasant, matter-of-fact tone and seemed to have a cordial, yet boundary-driven relationship with the incarcerated individuals. "Last names only."

That rule hadn't gone over well with Bruce. "They call you by your *last* name?" he'd asked during a Skype chat. He was worried that the repetition of "Woodford" over and over for weeks on end by male, maximum-security prison inmates might make me easily *findable* on the outside. "Is that safe? I mean, what's wrong with *Laurie*?" He'd looked at me with wounded eyes, the same sad expression he, most likely, imagined having at my funeral, the one where the few parts left of me had been poured into a pint-sized casket.

I wasn't concerned. If one of the incarcerated individuals was willing to lose early parole to put out a hit on someone, I figured he'd have bigger fish to fry than me. The only thing I might do to tick off one of these men might be suggesting he improve the structure and pacing of his personal essay. No inmate, I reasoned, would be willing to spend another ten years in the slammer to avenge hurt feelings over that. Presumably incarcerated individuals grew thicker skins than your average workshop student.

I stepped beside the chair that Coleman had slid from beneath the classroom's table and stacked my handouts and reams of writing paper on the table's surface. "Thank you,

Coleman," I said, taking a seat. I wore black slacks, a buttoned-up cotton shirt, rubber-soled dress shoes and no jewelry. Prison had plenty of rules, many of which pertained to attire. I could wear only close-toed shoes, for example; sandals were prohibited. And I couldn't wear an underwire bra since it might set off the metal detector. No form-fitting clothing or revealing necklines. No Spandex, no Lycra, no skirt worn above the knee. No headband, scarf, or metal hairpins. Upon arrival, the contents of my briefcase would be thoroughly searched. And under no circumstances were cell phones allowed inside the prison.

On workshop days, I secured my cell phone in the glove box of my car. On that particular morning, after pulling my car into the expansive prison lot -- dim gray and potholed -- my mother called to talk about Thanksgiving plans. "Do you have a minute?" my mother asked.

"I just pulled into the prison parking lot," I told her. "But I'm here early, so I have time."

"Okay, I'll be quick," my mother said. "You mentioned driving here for Thanksgiving?" I'd planned to make the six-hour drive from Ohio to upstate New York to visit relatives for the holiday. "Are you sure you want to do that?" she asked. "You know there can be weather this time of year." My mother was a "white knuckle" driver and "nervous flyer" who ended most conversations between the months of October and April with two words: "weather permitting."

"It's been a mild November," I said, gazing toward the prison entrance and the formidable wire fence, capped with spirals of barbed wire, that enclosed the prison's perimeter. "Besides," I continued, "I'll get on the road right after my prison class on Wednesday morning, so I'll be driving in daylight..."

"You know there are deer this time of year," she cautioned. In her emails, my mother had detailed the hazards faced by unwitting motorists when deer bound across roads and highways. According to my mother, at any given moment during my drive to New York, I risked becoming the blood-covered victim of a fawn-faced, doe-eyed killing machine.

For my mother, at times, navigating daily life was like wading through a steaming pool of jeopardy. Unpredictability and potential hazard offered themselves up at any given juncture. Yet she seemed unfazed by me teaching ten male inmates in a classroom accompanied by one prison official -- Jan, a clerk without a weapon. On workshop days, Jan sat at the corner desk jotting lists in her notebook, as I sat at the conference table alongside the incarcerated individuals. As I talked about writer's voice and word choice in their personal narratives, Jan wrote her Christmas list and weighed the pros and cons of serving chestnut stuffing versus plain for Thanksgiving dinner. If a problem were to arise with the inmates, the best Jan could do, it seemed, would be to make a note of it, or perhaps pen someone in the thigh. It wasn't that I wanted my mother, a self-professed "worrier," to fret. But you'd think, when it came to anxiety fodder, that me sitting wedged between maximum security prisoners each week might top dog a six-hour drive on toll roads in my Toyota Corolla.

I supposed Bruce was doing enough worrying for the both of them. "So there's no guard in your classroom," he'd said, expressing concern over what he saw as "inadequate security." Our prison classroom was located in a corridor with the dentist's office and chapel. The wall separating these rooms from the corridor was floor to ceiling security glass. At the end of the hallway sat an armed guard, who presumably had a direct view as well as video monitors of activity on the second floor.

There may have been an alarm button in the classroom – somewhere -- that Jan could have pushed between reading *Not Your Typical Stove Top* and *101 Christmas Gifts You Can Make from Tube Socks.*

In the classroom, the incarcerated individuals took their seats quickly, ready to get started. "Good morning, gentlemen," I said. "Any questions from last week's class?"

"Ah, Woodford…" Williams twisted his head slowly from left to right. "Where *do* you find these stories?" Smiling, he laughed through his teeth, a staccato kee, kee, kee escaping like a gas station air pump topping off a bicycle tire.

"I assume you're talking about the Sedaris essay?" I said. "Good choice. Right?"

"Ah, Woodford." Kee, kee, kee.

For a change of pace from Maya Angelou, Tobias Wolff, and Richard Wright, I chose to include David Sedaris' *Big Boy*, a delightfully hilarious essay set at an Easter Sunday get-together where the narrator excuses himself to use the host's bathroom where he finds a giant, flush-resistant turd floating in the toilet. After repeated, ineffective attempts to flush the human byproduct, the narrator scrambles, panicked, when another dinner guest knocks on the door to use the bathroom.

"Let's start with characterization," I suggest.

"The primary character," Robinson says, "is the turd itself."

"Not the narrator?" I ask.

"I think we learn more about the turd," Harris pipes in. "Author says turd is big as a burrito." The room erupts in laughter. "No toilet paper, nothin'!"

"And it won't flush down. Just spins round and round."

Kennedy leans forward, soft-spoken and reflective. "Maybe the narrator's the main character. I mean, he's *embarrassed* that someone will think it's *his*…"

"Yeah, the fool went ahead and told everyone he be back. He goin' to the bathroom…" Heads nod.

"Yeah, but end of paragraph one," Harris points to his handout, "the turd is all trembling and shi…" He side-eyes me. "Uh, sorry, Woodford…all trembling and *stuff*."

"Maybe turd *afraid* of bein' flushed," Williams adds. Kee. Kee. Kee. "Like when we talk about personification. Turd is personified."

"Turd so personified, the man be talking to it. Tellin' turd, 'Go on! Shoo!' like he talking to some kid..."

"Author talks to himself too," Harris adds. "Tells himself it ain't technically his job to get rid of that thing…"

"Yes," I interject. "Sedaris uses internal dialogue."

"Talking to himself. Talking to turd." Harris shakes his head. "Bottom line is, he don't want that stank pinned on him."

In Ohio, when I told people I was teaching at a prison, a recurring question from friends and relatives began with: *Maximum security…What did they do?* I couldn't answer that question because I didn't care. I was there to talk writing with these men, to engage in enthusiastic discussions about theme and syntax, to offer them an opportunity to read literary pieces not housed in their prison library and to read and respond to their own written work. Besides, why were their tarnished pasts any of my business? It wasn't as if I shared with them all the times that I was a lousy friend or bitchy to my ex-husband.

At the prison, while wrapping up our class discussion on the Sedaris essay, I asked, "What else? Any thoughts about plot, style?"

Coleman leaned forward with bright, syrup-brown eyes. "He talk about the whole event like it's a crime scene."

"Yeah," Williams agreed, "he don't want that turd pinned on him, but the problem is, he made his whereabouts known public."

"And when the woman knocks on the bathroom door, he considers a *cover up*," Kennedy said. "Maybe he'll wash his hair in the sink to cover up how much time he's in there," he added, smoothing his hand over a short-shorn patch of graying hair.

Harris nodded. "Afterwards, he goes out to the party to *examine the suspects* to find out who responsible."

"Suspense," Kennedy added. "The writer is building suspense. That's what he's doin'."

"Yeah, we all wonderin' will that thing flush or not..."

Williams shrugged. "That thing ain't goin' nowhere."

Essays written by the incarcerated individuals, themselves, were written with energy, rhythm, and raw description. "For next week," I'd tell them, "write an essay in first person about an 'Oh, shit!' moment." Or I'd say, "As you're working on your essay this week, pay special attention to incorporating vivid description, engage the five senses." The men arrived in the classroom, assignments thoroughly completed. Each read his work aloud with palpable passion. Their characters were tall, dark, and aggressive, wore hats cocked to the side and pounced on any sign of weakness. They read about Pop working the crowd and Tashika working her boyfriend -- her arms wrapped around his neck while she's seated, percolating, on his lap. They wrote stories fraught with compelling tension – a young son watching a drug dealer press a gun to his father's head, a teenager running away from her heroin-addicted mother, a sister abused by gang bangers. Their essays pulsed with gun fire, street banter and motorcycles backfiring.

Throughout the workshop, there was occasional mention of the inmates' siblings doing time in other correctional facilities, their "old man" serving time as well. They talked about mothers, sisters, cousins addicted to crack or meth or alcohol. Many, as children, had uncles or stepfathers who'd knocked them around, grandmothers or aunts who'd beaten them. Familial perpetrators caught in tailspins created by their own personal stories filled with grief, dejection, blind rage. After reading their essays, some of the gentlemen chuckled, shaking their heads. "Yeah, just the way it was. One minute, we havin' a party and the next, bullets flyin'…" I was left wondering, in such circumstances, just how much control one truly has to design his own narrative, to develop his character fully by story's end.

As youths, some turned away from biological family members to join their own flammable family of peers. "Man, Jimmy and I were tight. He was more of a brother than my own brother..." Now, standing in the chow hall line for canned beans and baloney sandwiches, waiting on a pass to see the prison chaplain or dentist, marking time during inmate count, they appeared to move through each day just trying to stay afloat, longing for release. For a few, reading and writing offered some measure of escape. "Gives me something to think about, something to concentrate my mind on. Better than thinking about bein' here." Writing personal essay or memoir – each having the chance to "tell my story" -- seemed especially cathartic, a distraction from their current circumstance of entrapment, a rescue of the psyche, of sorts.

Perhaps, occasionally, as they stood in their cell blocks during lockdown or paced the prison courtyard at allotted times -- living by the rules, living by the clock -- they contemplated the days when they'd moved through life with comrades. A time when they'd given one another heads ups, covered one another's backs, like a murder of crows perched atop a telephone wire, watchful and ready, waiting to fly.

SOMEWHERE ELSE

I was halted in the airport security line by a TSA officer. He wore a blue uniform and made a weird sucking sound as he breathed open mouthed. "Can't pass these through, Ma'am," he said, raising my round-tip scissors – the ones I trimmed my nose hair with -- up for inspection. I rolled my eyes. *You think I could hijack a plane with those things?* "Next time put 'em in checked baggage." I had no bag to check, no security-approved place to pack normal-sized shampoo or a corkscrew or, in this case, nose hair scissors. I had only carry-on. I was flying from my place in Ohio to visit Bruce in Oklahoma. A three-day weekend. The officer tossed my scissors into a bin. Confiscated.

This got under my skin. As did having to remove my shoes and walk through the metal detector in sweaty socks just because some maniac many years ago had gotten the bright idea to put explosive devices in his hiking boot. *Thanks a lot.* I gathered my laptop, sneakers and Ziplocked moisturizer bottles from rolling plastic containers on the security belt. Ugh. The joys of being in a long-distance relationship. I was tired of stuffing folded jeans and T-shirts into my backpack. Sick of cramming rolled socks and underwear into side pouches and zippered compartments. I'd had enough of sitting on turbulent aircrafts, my seatbelt buckled low and tight.

Throughout the semester, Bruce and I saw one another regularly, about every three weeks. Friends and colleagues said our relationship must be *serious*. Making that kind of effort. Flying up in the sky, like birds, in a plane. We were Super Daters.

After years of living as a divorcee, traveling the world by myself and relishing the autonomy, theoretically, Bruce and I had the relationship of my dreams. In Toledo, I had space -- workweek freedom to go about my life without explanation. I was under no obligation to send a text if I were staying in my office late. No need to leave a note on the kitchen countertop accounting for where I'd gone. No raised eyebrows when I ate nachos for dinner or waxed my upper lip while watching HGTV.

The tradeoff for such freedom, however, felt hectic. Frantically tying up loose ends at work to make my Friday flight or retrieve Bruce from the airport. Answering emails at boarding gates. Grading student papers on airplane seat trays. Mostly, it felt sad. That series of airport hugs and kisses, of until-next-times and goodbyes.

My lingering sadness was curious to me. Was I losing my edge? In the past, the enticement of moving on to the next thing, the next place softened the sting of farewells. With Bruce, I was no longer able to shake off our goodbye kisses by the time I walked through Concourse B on my way to somewhere else.

"This long-distance thing is hard," I told Bruce. We were Skyping. He was wearing a black cotton bathrobe with a frayed neckline. I was in a light blue nightgown dotted with chocolate ice cream stains.

"I really miss you," he said.

"I miss you too." My teaching semester was nearing its end. We'd planned for me to arrive in Stillwater just before Christmas and stay until the end of January. "Our month together will help," I told him.

"Four weeks isn't long enough," Bruce said.

Bruce had lived in Stillwater for thirty years and held a tenured position at his university. I was a college lecturer who signed a renewal contract each year.

Bruce had an idea.

"Cakes," he said. "You're leaving for China mid-February, right?"

"Right."

"And you're going back to Toledo two weeks beforehand to…?"

"Gather my teaching materials and pack up my stuff."

Bruce knit his eyebrows. "You return from China the end of May, right?"

"Uh, huh."

"And you go back to Toledo to…?"

"Unpack my stuff."

Bruce swallowed hard. "At my university, the English department is always scrounging to find enough qualified instructors to teach English Comp. during Fall semester."

I pinched my chin. "Okay..."

"Here's a thought." Bruce beamed. "Just move down here with me!"

*

For nearly fifty years, I'd identified as a northerner. Yet, at the end of fall semester in Toledo, after grading my last student paper, I stuffed all my belongings into my Toyota Corolla and drove 930 miles to relocate to Stillwater, Oklahoma.

Culture shock: *A sense of confusion and uncertainty sometimes with feelings of anxiety that may affect people exposed to an alien culture or environment without adequate preparation* (Merriam-Webster).

Oklahoma: *I Love My Truck* bumper stickers. *Skip Rope Not Church* key chains. Billboards advertising: *Calf Fries – The New Sac Lunch.* Velveeta talked up as a fine cheese (It's so creamy!).

I had so many questions.

What is chicken fried steak? (Answer: Steak fried and battered like fried chicken.)

What does "might could" mean? As in "Yes, ma'am. I might could get those copies to you by Wednesday." (Answer: Maybe. Maybe not.)

Locals would ask me, "Now, just whereabouts are you from?" New York, I'd tell them and they'd nibble on a hang nail and say, "Now, that explains a thing or two."

A question began knocking, no, lightly tapping, at my brain: What was I thinking?

To me, everything in Oklahoma appeared huge. Its fist-sized cowboy belt buckles. Its Dodge Rams with extra cabin space. Golf ball-sized hail. Bison heads mounted above fireplaces. Two-story tall Life Church crosses. 24-ounce Ribeyes. My growing anxiety.

I tried positivity. Talked up Oklahoma's mild winters. Said things like, "and the people here are so friendly!" Yet, when it came to living in the Sooner State, I harbored a real attitude. I sized up everything Oklahoman with scrutiny – its restaurants, parks, health care practitioners. I might admit that my doctor in Oklahoma was fine. But up north, I'd quickly add, I had an amazing general practitioner. I might concede that Stillwater's *Eskimo Joe's* served decent burgers. But in New York, I could get great burgers *and* ethnic food. In my mind, anything Oklahoma could do, the north could do better. I was like a discontented wife comparing her husband to past lovers, and Oklahoma routinely came up with clumsy hands and a less than adequate appendage.

Hoping that community service would be a path forward to warming up to my new environment, I applied to teach a creative writing class at a men's medium-security prison in rural Oklahoma. I packed a canvas bag with student handouts and notebooks with wire-free binding. Then went off to prison.

Much of the soil in Oklahoma is red clay and loam, yet the prison compound, with its sparsely grassed yard and tired, brick buildings, appeared as washed out as a pale face in a beige turtleneck. The inmates looked as colorless as their landscape. Several men were elderly or at least seemed elderly with dull grey hair, bony bodies, creased foreheads.

My writing workshop was held in a community room and scheduled to start after a theatre group workshop run by Shari, a lithe woman in her fifties with a delicate face and short, cropped hair as if she'd taken a role on stage starring in *Peter Pan*. Shari had invited me to help the inmates develop their writing skills in order to produce scripts for plays they'd later act out. "Most of the men are very creative in acting out a story," Shari explained. "But the script writing poses a real challenge." Shari was compassionate, quick-witted and had built a strong rapport with the group. When she turned a chunk of class time over to me, the men's eyes deadened with disappointment, like kids being forced to spend a weekend with the unfun grandparent.

The class consisted of twenty or so inmates who sat at rectangular tables in a horseshoe configuration. Most of my workshop attendees were White. They sat quietly with slumped shoulders and moist eyes while I distributed handouts of brief, published essays that incorporated vivid description and effective dialogue. "Thank you, Ma'am. God bless," they mumbled when I placed the packets in front of them. Like strep throat spreading through a college dorm, these men seemed to have caught the low-brewing depression that was going around the prison. "God bless you, Ma'am."

I supposed many of us, when faced with the rock bottom of imprisonment might seek comfort in a higher power. Being locked up without access to drugs, alcohol or *Jerry Springer*, the vast majority of these men had apparently found God.

For a Jesus seeker, Oklahoma was the place to be. Stillwater, with a population of around 50,000 residents, boasted well over sixty churches – First Southern Baptist Church, Living Waters, Bible Missionary, Church of the First Born. It wasn't uncommon to hear a checkout clerk at Rite Aid slide in a "Have a blessed day!" Or to read a message doodled on a bathroom stall door exclaiming, "Jesus loves you!" At any given juncture phrases like, "God bless you" and "You're in my prayers" were doled out from stranger to stranger like beans and wieners at a church picnic.

On Oklahoma country roads, along hot stretches of melting asphalt and crepe myrtle, I'd read town billboards expounding messages like, "God is the answer" and "Jesus saves." Posted in Perkins township, one billboard declared, "Jesus is Lord over Perkins." I scratched my head. Yeah, but who's the mayor?

I held up my handout. "Let's start by reading an essay entitled, 'Lights,'" I began. I read Dybek's three-paragraph, evocative vignette aloud then asked, "Where does this scene take place?" The inmates stared at their handouts. I read the vignette again. "Where is the narrator -- the person telling the story -- in this scene?" Silence. "Is he in a rural area, in the country?"

"No, Ma'am," said Honeywell. "I think he's in the city."

"Good," I said. "How do we know?"

Honeywell leaned his forehead into his palm. "Ma'am, he's watching cars."

"Yes, there's traffic. Anything else that tells us he's in a city or neighborhood?"

"Yes, Ma'am," said Dunkirk, who's in his thirties, I'd guess. He had a chiseled jaw, almond eyes. High school football captain cute. Only he looked tired, worn as his former team's end-of-season pig skin. "It says there's a storefront."

"Yes, good, a storefront and there's mention of 'all down the block' there's yelling from doorways… Are there words or descriptions in this essay that jump out at you? That you like?" I waited. "For example," I said, "I like the description toward the end '…voices winking on like fireflies.' Anything that you like?"

"Ma'am," Honeywell began, "I like the somewhere else part." He traced his calloused finger along the page and read, "That glide to somewhere else." The other inmates nodded. That was their favorite line too, they said.

I asked the gentlemen to write their own "Lights." A scene from their lives in three paragraphs. "Sift through scenes in your past or recent memories," I told them. "Then try to describe it as vividly as possible." Holding their pens, they stared down at blank paper. "Sometimes it helps," I suggested, "to start with freewriting." They began to scrawl.

The vignettes the inmates produced read like a tire gone low. In bedraggled voices, they expressed appreciation for their loved ones on the outside. Nostalgia for their former lives. Hopes for redemption. Wistful memories of holiday meals served on real plates – turkey and mashed potatoes piled high on Grandma's fancy china -- rather than on the plastic compartment meal trays they took from stacks in the prison cafeteria.

"Fond memories of home," I said. The gentlemen nodded.

At the age of fifty-three, having visited Stillwater many times, I'd made a conscious decision to move in with Bruce. Yet I felt plagued by an overpowering sense of not fitting in. Something as routine as a dental appointment would serve as a reminder of culture clash and leave me feeling convinced that I just didn't belong.

"Laurie? This is Suzy from Dr. Ferguson's office again." Suzy had called the day before to remind me of the dental cleaning I'd scheduled. I'd managed to fit it in just before my semester in China. "That's right, me again." Suzy said. "I guess I just like talkin' to ya." She chuckled into the phone. "Anyways, Miss Laurie, would it be possible to change your appointment time? Say, to one o'clock?"

"Sure, that would be fine," I said, but ended up rushing into the dental office, apologizing for being five minutes late. "Oh, don't *you* apologize to us," Suzy assured me. "You did us a favor comin' early."

My hygienist, Kaytee, was equally nice. "Whatever you're doing at home is workin'," Kaytee said. "Gums look healthy.

Why, there's hardly anything here for me to scrape off." Kaytee chatted to put clients at ease. She asked carefully timed questions that I could briefly answer between saliva-suctioning and gum-scraping with her silver curette.

I learned about Kaytee's young daughter who'd become angry when her friend, Piper, said that her feet were tiny. *They are not tiny!* Kaytee's daughter had said and Kaytee had told her daughter, "You know, it's no fun having big feet. Piper is probably jealous. And, by the way, young lady, you just be grateful for how God made you."

Sitting in the chair with my Cape Cod blue bib chained around my neck, I smiled around Kaytee's latex-gloved hand. Then the topic turned to office morale.

"There are nine *women* in this office," Kaytee said. "So, as you can imagine, we have our moments." I gave an open-jawed swallow as she continued. "There was a time we had our little estrogen clashes, you know how women are, but now we really all get along." Kaytee added, "Amazing, really. Nine women in one office and we get along."

People still say that? I thought. *Out loud? To other women?* I wondered about the level of morale in the men's prisons where I'd taught, whether the male inmates housed in one complex also *had their moments.*

There's a difference between visiting a place and relocating there, I quickly realized. Just as there's a difference between staying at Bruce's house for, say, a long weekend and moving into it, like, indefinitely.

When it came to home furnishings, especially since I'd started traveling, I veered toward minimalism. Bruce, on the other hand, was a big fan of things. I'd noticed that previously, of course, when I visited his house on weekends. But then I'd head back to my tidy space in Fayetteville or Toledo and Bruce's clutter would become a distant memory.

As I walked through the living room on my way to the kitchen to set the table for dinner, I banged my thigh on the leg of Bruce's sofa. It was a brown leather bachelor sofa with reclining end sections that blubbered up half the living room like a whale washed ashore. Limping toward the kitchen, I mused, Was it the size of a Humpback? Orca? Narwhal? I held up a finger. "Sperm whale." Leaning against the countertop, I scanned the cupboards trying to remember where Bruce kept his plates and salad bowls.

Back when I lived in New York, I owned a set of colorful ceramic dishes featuring a mosaic design in bright blues, yellows, and greens. I hadn't paid much for them but was fond of their fun, artsy vibe.

Bruce's dishes had a different vibe altogether. On his saucers and bowls were hand painted horses, pigs, a boy in plaid pants tethering a kite. Bruce's dishes featured cows, sheep, a skirted farm girl standing beneath a mostly sunny sky. The bottoms of some bowls and mugs read, *The End.* Twelve full sets of these dishes occupied cupboards in Bruce's cramped kitchen, along with matching extras. Ceramic serving platters. Sugar bowl and creamer. Salt and pepper shakers. Dish soap dispensers. Each hand painted with agricultural trivia.

I opened one cupboard looking for plates but, instead, found stacks of mugs with a farmer's wife and quacking duck. "There's more," I whispered. I opened a deep drawer beneath the stovetop to find a bowl-to-serve-ten with painted Farmer holding a rake. Then another cupboard taken over by stacks of salad plates decorated with cud-chewing ruminants and a pitcher sporting a barn, silo, and flying crows. "More."

Bruce's house sat on a quiet, tree-lined lane. The clustered hardwoods in his backyard attracted flickers, hawks, barred owls. "Look!" Bruce would say. "That bird at the feeder! It's a red-bellied woodpecker."

"Yes, I see."

At night, Bruce and I would lay in bed listening to the barred owl's call. *WhoCooksForYou? WhoCooksForYou?*

"Listen, Cakes," Bruce would say, draping a warm arm across my belly. "It's Our Owl."

"Yes, I hear."

It was Our Owl, but His House. "It's a great house," I told Bruce. And meant it. But I disliked the Santa Fe-style wallpaper in the downstairs bath. Was it Terracotta? Salamander Orange? And all the green. The green! Painted on the walls of the living room. Dining room. Foyer. Bruce told me that the paint color was Pine. "More like Pickle," I said.

There were many rules to follow in Bruce's pickle-painted house. They were gently expressed by a patient Bruce but were rules just the same. When it came to laundry, Bruce advocated a five-basket system. A basket for towels, for whites, for brights, for clothes to wash in warm, for clothes washed on gentle cycle. "Add a capful of The Laundress for delicates," Bruce instructed. "Woolite Darks for anything that fades." It was imperative, Bruce explained, to have an extra rinse cycle for all loads. And bleach should be added to the water when washing towels. Bruce opposed moldiness.

When using the dishwasher, plastic containers must never go on the bottom rack. Tall glasses go on the top rack in the back. Knives and salad bowls, handwashed only. Some evenings, Bruce would watch me stack the dishwasher and comment, "One might consider securing the measuring cups by the holes in their handles." Or, "One could stack wine glasses more efficiently in the row adjacent to the coffee mugs."

"You mean, *you* could?" I'd ask. "*You* could do that?"

Because I sure as hell wasn't about to.

I sat on the examination table, my new Stillwater physician tapping my knee with a rubber mallet. He ran his ungloved hands down my legs, over my ankles, checking for edema. "Strong calves," he said. "Good for you." He was a year older than me and talked about the importance of routine exercise for folks our age. "Keep up the good fight," he told me. His teeth were unnaturally white. The skin along his temples appeared pulled tight. Were those hair plugs? Later, as he pressed a stethoscope at the bottom of my ribcage, I blurted out, "I think I should start back on anti-depressants."

"Breathe," the doctor told me.

That afternoon, back at the house, I ate yogurt out of the farmer's wife bowl while sitting on the reclining whale sofa. My eyes scanned the room cluttered with Bruce's furniture and knick-knacks, his spider plants, and electronics. My spoon scraped bottom. *The End,* said the bowl.

In the bedroom, I set my largest suitcase on the window seat. Counted and packed work slacks and blouses. Sweaters and shawls. Later, Bruce entered the room. "Your China trip is still three weeks away," he reminded me, staring at my luggage.

"It's never too early to get organized," I said. And I breathed.

GOING THE DISTANCE

I thought that getting out of Stillwater for a while might do both Bruce and me some good, yet my body itched with apprehension at the thought of getting on the plane.

The night before my trip, our power went out. I'd awoken to pitch blackness, my eyes darting in the direction of the digital clock Bruce kept on the dresser that, on other nights, luminated the hours and minutes in a Mars red glow. That night, nothing. I searched for the sliver of light that generally shown through the bedroom blinds from distant streetlights but encountered a wall of darkness. Not even moonlight. In my half-asleep state, I decided I'd gone blind. That I'd somehow detached a retina, snapped an optic nerve. Could that happen? Instantaneous blindness. Could that be a thing? My first concern was, how would I read and write? Braille. Audiobooks. Voice-recognition. Then, how would I travel? Get from one place to another? White cane. Guide dog. Holding onto another person's arm.

At the airport, I wrapped my arms around Bruce's waist, intertwined my fingers at the small of his back and held on for a very long time. "I miss you already," I said.

For the entirety of my three-month stay in Hangzhou, my university put me up in the Xiang Yao Hotel -- a twelve-story establishment with a cavernous, chandeliered lobby located near the Quiantang River. "Paradise" was how a former Chinese colleague once described Hangzhou, a city in China's Zhejiang province with a population of about six million. Hangzhou was known for its silk industry and artsy culture since the area attracted numerous painters and writers. Tourists were drawn to the aesthetic beauty of Hangzhou's quaint vicinity called West Lake with its temples and arched bridges and pagodas amidst lotus gardens. The Xiang Yao Hotel was a forty-five-minute subway ride from paradisiacal West Lake and located in, what felt to me like, a colorless expanse of suburban sprawl.

I busied myself with strategic settling in. Everyday toiletries organized on the bathroom countertop; the remainder set underneath the sink. Umbrella and rain jacket tucked in the closet corner. Electronics and teaching materials stored in desk drawers. From a street vendor, I bought laundry soap, a plastic bin for handwashing underwear, socks, T-shirts and an aluminum drying rack. I stored them beneath the bed. I stacked bottled water and snacks in the cupboard below the television that broadcast one channel in English. I was pleased with my aptitude for one-room living.

Outdoors, I crossed crowded intersections, walked past vast grids of grey, concrete-slabbed twenty-story apartment buildings and businesses. I passed on the sidewalk, a group of men, in black slacks, button-down shirts and chef hats, smoking cigarettes. Two of them were picking their noses as if finger-diving for gold. *Were those the guys who prepared my Dongpo pork last night?*

I expected to feel bright and clear-headed in China, but instead my mood was drab.

Was I bored? Aspects of Asian culture I'd found fascinating upon moving, years earlier, to South Korea now struck me as same old. Grocery stores stocked with shrimp-flavored potato chips; restaurant water tanks filled with horseshoe crab and eels; grown men driving electric scooters draped with Hello Kitty wind quilts; McDonald's delivery men on motorcycles speeding down side streets with Big Mac packs. I was done taking photos of sea anemone in glass tanks at WuMart. I'd seen it, lived with it, all before. Yawn.

There's a saying in Zen Buddhism that goes something like this: *If you walk around with a little piece of shit on your nose, everywhere you go, it will stink.* Zen's answer: *Wash your face.*

I'd head out with a focus on the beauty around me. In city parks, grandmothers danced in synchronized steps to flutes and violas. Cascading notes in sharps and flats. Along the Hangzhou River, children flew kites – garnet-red dragons, pink butterflies, saffron Phoenixes. Their parents cooked skewered pork over charcoal grills. I passed a woman holding an infant and decided that Chinese babies were absolutely the cutest babies in the world. Wispy black hair and circle-pink cheeks. Panda cub look-alikes without the undereye circles. Yet, a few moments later, my mind latched onto darkness once again. The crowds of sidewalk people dressed in black, in coats the color of lead. Pollution obscuring bluer skies. Hulk like architecture reminding us we're small. I was but a mere speck, floating ash.

Before Bruce visited Hangzhou, he was under the false impression that everyday tasks were simple to accomplish. "Your sink is clogged? Just call down to the front desk," he'd say during one of our video WeChat conversations. "Tell them you need a maintenance person." I'd remind him that no one at the front desk spoke English. Bruce would pause, then say, "There has to be *someone.*"

During our chats, Bruce and I talked a lot about food. What will you have for dinner tonight? was a standard question. I'd mention one or two places that I frequented, restaurants that had menus with pictures. "Again?" Bruce would say. "You don't feel like trying a new place?" I'd tell him that I needed the pictures to know what I was ordering. Then admit that I could make more of an effort. I could flip through pages of my Chinese – English translation book, point at words, mime my desires. But it all felt like such a bother. "Just ask for an English menu," Bruce would suggest, and I'd explain that most restaurants didn't have one. Bruce would shake his head. "They must keep their English menus *somewhere.*"

A day or two before Bruce arrived, I worried he'd Boy-Up my tidy room. I imagined his shirts and giant man-pants draped on my desk chair, his books and magazines cluttering my countertops.

It seemed that, when a glass of water was placed on a nightstand and Bruce was nearby, the glass would soon be knocked over. The same went for shallow dishes of soy sauce on tabletops and cups of coffee on desk corners. For some reason whenever Bruce emerged from the bathroom, floor linoleum and Formica countertops were pooled with water. Bruce washed up like a wren in a bird bath. Always splashing.

When Bruce did arrive in Hangzhou, all my petty concerns instantly disappeared. Bruce had finagled work schedules, tapped into savings, spent sixteen hours on cramped airplane seats and endured jetlag to visit me. I wrapped my arms around his waist, buried my face in his neck. "It's you! You're here!" I cried, my heartbeat racing with happiness.

In China, Bruce spoke English loudly. "Yelling words doesn't help," I'd tease. Then I'd hear him shouting -- "Boneless chicken?" -- to a shrugging grocery clerk and yelling -- "Electric plug adapter?" – at a vendor in a Shanghai market.

When Bruce was a little boy, his father, who'd volunteered for a non-profit organization in post-war China, had taught Bruce a few Chinese words. Simple standard greetings. Bruce's favorite word was Nihao, which meant hello. His father told him it's pronounced like a cat meowing. Meow. Nihao. Meow. Nihao. Little Bruce had practiced.

One afternoon, in the Xiang Yao elevator, the doors opened on the fourth floor. Two teenage girls stepped in. "Nihao," Bruce meowed. The girls froze for a moment, brushed strands of long black hair behind their ears, then burst into laughter. They laughed all the way to the first floor, still giggling as they rushed through the lobby.

Bruce was a big fan of the breakfast buffet at the Xiang Yao hotel. "Six different kinds of dumplings," he said. "Six! And I have no idea what this black seaweedy thing is, but it's delicious!" I watched him, from across our table, pinching food with chopsticks, chewing with great concentration while I drank coffee and ate toast with jam. Back in our room, Bruce pored over the menu of the restaurant I liked, the one with pictures of some of their entrees and appetizers labeled in poorly translated English. "Look," Bruce said, chuckling. "The first dish listed under the *Healthy Vegetables* column is *Oil Residue Spinach*. And there's a dish called, *Do You Want To Eat My Tofu?*"

At that restaurant, Bruce and I ordered *Crazy Corn* assuming we'd be served a vegetable. The waiter brought ice cream with syrup. I'd long since tired of these linguistical follies. But Bruce took it all in stride. "This is awesome!" Bruce said, after our entrées arrived. "Who knew that bullfrog came with bones!"

I took a bite and smiled. "China is more colorful when you're around."

One night, Bruce and I sat on the king-sized bed, backs against the pillowed headrest, in my sixth-floor hotel room with modern amenities. The Xiang Yao created an ambiance of faux elegance. Walls papered in ebony and dull gold. Black-veneered wardrobes and nightstands. "Fancy," one of my Chinese colleagues had called it. The Xiang Yao's hallways were carpeted in iron gray and by late afternoon a nimbostratus of cigarette smoke hovered beneath its ceilings. With every light switch flipped to "on," my room remained as dark as the back corridor of an adult bookstore.

"You're sure you want to come to work with me tomorrow?" I asked Bruce. I was scheduled to teach and hold office hours for a four-hour block. Bruce planned to join me. He'd bring a book, he said, and drink instant coffee and probably doze off on the black vinyl futon in my office while I was in class. I welcomed his company but had a concern. "What if, you know…"

Bruce perked his head. "Oh," he began, his brows furrowing. "I just won't." Bruce was referring to an anatomical function – referred to in preschools as "number two" -- that would be problematic, for him, at the university where I taught. A university that housed only squat toilets. If nature called, I reminded him, he may not have a choice in the matter. Bruce sunk his feet in. "Not gonna happen."

"Sweetie," I began, "You'll be at my college all morning long and into the afternoon..." Bruce shook his head, tensing red-faced and rigid like a three-year-old refusing to put on pajamas. "Drinking coffee after all that Kungpao chicken and red pepper spinach you ate tonight…"

"Just won't do it."

When Bruce and I first met, my travel experience was something he'd fawned over a bit. "The Adventurer," he called me. The current reality of travel for Bruce – navigating toilet logistics in a far-off land – suddenly seemed more worrisome than adventuresome.

I offered Bruce some global perspective. "People have pooped in holes for centuries," I said. "By the way, Asians probably think we're disgusting. Squishing our bare behinds against the same seat as everyone else in the bathroom queue." Bruce shrugged. I continued, "I'm just saying, you may want to think through a just-in-case scenario."

"Oh, I lived that scenario years ago during a trip to India," Bruce said.

"And you lived to tell about it."

"I was in my twenties then." Bruce glanced down at his 62-year-old legs. "With hip flexors a whole lot more bendable and still…" His voice cracked. It was true; Bruce was no Russian gymnast. The last time he'd tried to sit cross-legged on the floor, he tipped all the way backward like a heavy-headed baby.

"But you figured it out, right?"

"I had to take my pants off – all the way off -- so I wouldn't drop a brick in my jeans."

"Unpleasant, I'll give you that," I acknowledged. Since my stay in China stretched out much longer than Bruce's ten-day visit, I figured I outranked him in complaining rights. "How do you think I feel? I have girl parts. I have to squat every time. *Every time.* And I'm here for twelve weeks. The other day I accidentally tilted to the left and peed on my shoe."

I had no real right to complain. My university treated me well. They'd put me up in a nice-enough hotel, provided a meal card, and invited me to lunches with the Dean. Dishes of Longjing shrimp, Chongqing noodles, baked fish in vinegar all served on a rotating, circular table the circumference of a tractor tire. My students were diligent and engaged, and my kind Chinese colleagues practically shook with concentration while communicating politely with me in their stilted English. But being confronted by my otherness was unavoidable. When I walked down a college corridor or entered the main office, faculty members' and students' eyes dilated, heads turned – *foreigner in the building!*

I patted Bruce's arm. "Sorry," I said. "Your bathroom business is really none of my business."

"Don't worry about me," Bruce said. "If anything moves down my digestive tract while I'm there, it'll just have to prairie dog until we're back at the hotel."

It felt a bit cringe-worthy for Bruce to bring burrowing rodents from the prairie into the toilet conversation, but he was from Oklahoma.

In China, ogling foreigners seemed to be considered good sport. Pointing, giggling, and guffawing were all fair play. A few weeks earlier while riding the subway in Hangzhou, the car doors swooshed open at the Yun Shui stop and an older woman with permed hair and veiny hands stepped on. She was under five-foot-tall and carried on her back a pie-faced, preschool-aged grandchild who appeared gargantuan by comparison. I noticed this often in China and Korea. Due to improved access to food and proper nutrition over the past fifty years, it was not uncommon to see a tiny, hunched grandmother carrying a "baby" the size and weight of a mini fridge. With the subway car in motion, the woman staggered to the empty seat beside mine, turned around so her back faced the seat, then deposited the kid, like a sand truck dumping a load.

It wasn't long before I sensed their gazes, sharp and fixed, in my direction. The grandmother and child pointed at me, giggling. Then they held up their hands – index fingers and thumbs touching, forming circles -- in front of their eyes. *Yes, okay,* I thought, my lips curving into a stupid grin. *The foreigner has round eyes.* Then came my nose. The grandmother placed her thumbnail at the end of her nose, then outstretched her index finger, indicating that my nose was the length of your average shoehorn. The grandmother and child smiled, chattering in Chinese. Round eyes, Long nose! I imagined them saying.

It was easier with Bruce around. Navigating sidewalks, subway lines and train stations with him by my side took some pressure off me. With Bruce's thick belly, full beard, hairy arms and neck, he proved the greater attraction. Passersby pointed at him. On the subway, teenage boys tried to touch Bruce's body hair, nonchalantly brushing the backs of their hands atop Bruce's forearms. Once, in Hangzhou's Lake District, I emerged from the ladies' room to find two older gentlemen, wearing Buddhist prayer beads, smiling broadly while rubbing Bruce's belly. "How could I say *no*?" Bruce said to me later. "They were such nice guys."

On my days off, Bruce and I walked around my neighborhood, bought dumplings from local vendors. A block from the Xiang Yao was an Optician's center that we passed almost daily. "It gets me every time," Bruce would say, laughing, pointing at the name of the optician's office spelled out on the storefront in large letters -- Helen Keller. Bruce had no qualms about looking like a tourist. He'd stand in subway cars flipping through pages in his China guidebook. "There's a Jewish Refugees Museum in Shanghai," he'd say. "And a wetland park here in Hangzhou." Some days we visited temples and gardens in Hangzhou or took the train to Shanghai. But the part I liked best was sitting on the bed in our dim hotel room with my head on Bruce's chest.

My teaching schedule in China was unconventional by American standards. I taught a three-hour section of English Composition on Sunday mornings in order to accommodate a complex maze of student schedules. My students often overloaded on courses to meet enrollment requirements for classes in their major, in addition to taking extra English courses to function linguistically in the U.S. My other classes were held at night. After other faculty and staff in the building had long since gone home, I sat in my office pouring hot drinking water from a kettle. Around 5:30 p.m., maintenance turned off building lights and everything went dark. The entryway, corridors, bathrooms, stairwells, classrooms. The first time that happened, I'd stepped out of my office and flicked the hall light back on. Within minutes, a maintenance man flicked it off again. My office was on the fifth floor of the building, my classroom on the third floor. At 6:30, I'd step into the black corridor, walk away from the glow of my office light, down the dark stairwell grasping the rail, feeling for each step with the toe of my shoe. No white cane. No guide dog. No one's arm to hold onto. I'd flick the lights on in classroom 316, stand in the doorway waiting for my students. They'd enter the dark building, illuminate their cell phones. *Winking on like fireflies*, I'd think.

In the classroom, students sat on little rectangular wooden stools placed six to a table. They rubbed their hands together, zipped their coats to their chins. "So cold!" they'd say. There was no central heat in the campus buildings. Only single heating units that stood in the backs of offices and classes like electronic room monitors. "How are you, Laurie teacher?"

"So cold," I'd tell them. Then add, "And so happy to see you."

The sun had not yet risen when Bruce's taxi arrived. We sat silent, hands on one another's knees, during much of the thirty-five-minute ride to the Hangzhou airport. I stood beside him at airline check-in. Sat with him on a hard bench postponing the inevitable. I guess it's time, we said, and I blew kisses as he disappeared behind the security partition.

On the ride back, I was convinced that my taxi driver had a death wish. Red-faced and grouper-mouthed, he swerved from lane to lane. Gunning past trucks. Tapping his brakes. *Seven more weeks,* I repeated like a mantra until his vehicle came to a stop in front of my campus and the driver jabbed a finger at the red numbers on his fare meter.

In class, I went over elements in a persuasive essay. Talked about a clearly defined thesis, strong evidential support, anecdotal evidence, emotional appeal. Students mentioned that I looked tired. "Dark circles," Chunhua said, pressing her fingers beneath her eyes.

"I was awake very early this morning," I told them. "Took Bruce to the airport. He's on his way back home."

"So sad!" they said. "You're all alone now."

"It's okay," I told them. "I'm good at being alone."

They shook their heads. "So sad."

After class, I sat in my de-cluttered hotel room. No big, belted pants flung on my desk chair, no magazines scattered on the desktop, no pools of water on the bathroom floor. I found Bruce's tube sock lying on the floor near the bed. Rather than tossing it into the dirty laundry bin, I left it there reminded of the day, many years ago, when I'd discovered my German Shepard's chew toy in the laundry room a week after he died and didn't have the heart to throw it away.

Days dragged on for me in China. Sloth-like, solitary. Other than my students, Bruce was about the only person I talked with. We video chatted my mornings, his evenings. Me, sitting on the hotel bed drinking instant coffee, my phone propped on the pillow. Bruce sitting on his sofa sipping hot tea. "I went to another Dean's lunch," I told him. "They served cold tea in cans with a straw."

"I attended another board meeting," Bruce said. "Managed to stay awake for most of it."

Sometimes when we ran out of things to say, I'd lift my T-shirt and flash my bra at his thumbnail screen face. He'd smile and tease, "Wanna see what I have under this longyi?" Then we'd talk about nothing again. I'd tell him I walked six miles along the Quiantang River. Stopped to watch the fishermen float their nets. Bruce would tell me that he saw Our Owl on a tree branch. Bought Geraniums for his front porch. It was our slow waltz. My lifeline.

Sometimes, after we ended our conversation, I'd stand in front of the window, watching damp laundry being wind dried on Chinese rooftops and wonder why I'd felt so disoriented in

Stillwater, Oklahoma. Why I'd been so peevish living in Bruce's warm house. Then I'd decide that it was those stupid dishes of his.

Take a Closer Look

Initially, it felt great being home. Back to clean air, blue skies, big green leafy salads, Bruce's open arms.

There were many things I admired about Bruce. His intelligence. Warmth. Patience. Kindness. Playfulness. Generosity. His thoughtfulness made me swoon. When Bruce learned about my digestive sensitivity to eggs, he immediately began triple-checking ingredients. "I'll make a revised beef stroganoff," he'd tell me. "Without the egg noodles, of course." He bought vegan mayonnaise, bakery breads sans egg wash, and egg-free salad dressings. Then I came home one evening to a freshly baked batch of brownies. He'd substituted Greek yogurt for eggs.

"Oh, my God. They were delicious," I told my mother.

"He's a keeper," my mother said.

As the weeks passed in Stillwater, however, a sense of longing emerged. I missed the relationships I'd cultivated in upstate New York. Spending time with Bruce was great, but I needed a friend. Another woman with whom I could join for a movie, or a walk, or meet for a glass of wine and talk about books, politics, annoying co-workers. While I tended toward introversion, making friends, I realized, would require effort -- getting out there, meeting people. I scanned Stillwater's township's calendar of events. The Botanic Garden was offering an Herb and Succulent Festival and the town library was sponsoring a workshop on insect-eating bats. There was Friday night Contradancing at the community center and, for pet lovers, the university was hosting Mutt Mondays and Waggin' Wednesdays. I liked plants and animals. I didn't like Contradancing, but what the hell. *Put yourself out there,* became my battle cry.

At events, I'd scan the room, approach any woman willing to make eye contact, introduce myself and strike up a conversation. I'd love to hear more about your work, I'd say. So, tell me about your family...your gardening...your Jack Russell Terrier. *You're trying too hard,* the voice inside my head warned as I smiled and nodded, shook hands and patted shoulders. *You're scaring them!* Before they darted away, I'd offer up my email address and cell phone number, suggest meeting for coffee some time. My phone remained quiet; my calendar bare.

A few months later, Bruce and I invited a couple over for dinner. I vacuumed the living room rug, wiped kitchen countertops, folded linen napkins, and made lasagna in hopes of bonding with the couple who were Bruce's old-time friends. The man was a mathematician who'd worked with Bruce since 1988. His wife was a set designer who'd known Bruce for over twenty years. The couple lived in Stillwater and owned a cabin in Colorado where Bruce and his ex-wife, Cathy, used to visit in the summer.

We sat on the whale sofa passing Bruce's plates, hand painted with poultry and mules and heaped with summer sausage, stinky cheese, and peppadews. I placed two pans of lasagna in the oven. One with meat, the other without. The set designer was vegetarian. I returned to the living room and listened as they reminisced about the week the four of them hiked near their cabin in Colorado in 1997. The fun math parties that Bruce and Cathy had hosted in this very house. I asked Bruce to pass the peppadews and accidentally called him by my ex-husband's name. It surprised me that "Larry" had slipped out with such ease. Then realized Bruce and I were playing husband and wife, hosting a couple's dinner in a house we both inhabited. No one seemed to notice the slip. The mathematician and set designer talked about their New Year's Eve party to which Bruce and Cathy had brought champagne and cake. I drank wine faster than the others. Checked the lasagnas again while the three of them pedaled their Flintstone car down memory lane. I offered more wine. Re-filled my glass. Then asked, "Is your Colorado cabin anywhere near Gunnison?"

Their eyebrows raised. They talked a bit about geography then. "You've been to Gunnison?"

"Oh, yes. Drove through a few years back when I stayed at a biological laboratory for a week."

"Biology? Don't you teach English?"

"At that time, I was in a relationship with a scientist," I said. "You know, past life."

I returned to the oven. Peeled back aluminum foil. *Will this pasta ever bubble?*

Around that time, I grew lonelier and less content by the day. I wanted local friends but felt disheartened by my failed attempts at making that happen. I wanted to share a life with Bruce but, with his life already so firmly established, felt incapable of carving out space.

I wanted to sleep soundly in a house that felt like home, but I found the bedroom in Bruce's house kind of creepy. I didn't say this to Bruce, but mentally listed the reasons why. The tarnished candle holders and dented water pitcher from Syria. Box-framed moths and butterflies pinned to cardboard. An old charcoal sketch of a grimacing man in a tall, tilted hat who reminded me of a killer clown. The floorboards that creaked. The swollen wooden door that didn't close completely and groaned open in the wee hours of the night.

My work situation in Stillwater didn't help matters. I'd hoped to secure a full-time teaching position but, instead, was hired as an adjunct, teaching four sections of International English Composition to college freshmen for low pay and no benefits.

Two days before classes started, I woke up with a boil under my left eyebrow. I smeared it with a gob of expired anti-acne gel I'd found in the back of Bruce's bathroom cupboard, willing it to miraculously disappear. Throughout the day, the boil expanded like porridge in a pot. Bruce drove me to Walgreens to look for an ointment he'd heard about, some magic boil-be-gone elixir. I scanned the aisles but couldn't find it. As consolation, I bought two boxes of Milk Duds and a bag of Swedish Fish and slid into the passenger's seat of Bruce's car.

On our way home, I looked in the visor mirror and gently touched the tender lump of red flesh. Bruce said, "Picking at it will only make it worse."

"I know, I know."

That night, after Bruce fell asleep, I tiptoed to the bathroom. Rummaged through a drawer for a safety pin and wiped its sharp tip with Rubbing Alcohol. I was an unqualified surgeon.

The next morning, Bruce turned to me, kissed my neck. In the daylight, he saw the boil. It was swollen, doubled in size, an angry red. I'd really pissed it off the night before. It was Sunday. In twenty-four hours, I'd stand at a podium facing classrooms filled with college freshmen. "Oh, Cakes," Bruce said.

Later, Bruce drove me to urgent care. "So, what's going on with your eye?" the physician's assistant asked. I confessed; she shook her head and waved for me to follow her. It'd take a few days for the antibiotics to clear the carnage. "In the meantime," the P.A. added, "don't pick at it."

That afternoon, seated at the country-style oak table that Bruce's ex-wife had left behind, I went over my lesson plans for the following morning. Bruce's kitchen clock, the one he'd gotten for Christmas in 2004, blared bird songs every hour. At two o'clock, a Purple Martin chirped. At three o'clock, American Goldfinches called. I stared at the pickle green walls feeling a deep sense of homesickness even though I no longer had any sense of where home was.

That night I drank too much wine and told Bruce that our relationship felt disjointed. His life, my life. "We do some things really well as a couple," I said, "but we have no shared vision." I noted Bruce's baffled expression. "I mean, really," I pressed. "What's our shared vision?" Bruce kissed my forehead. Retired to his creepy bedroom. I drank another glass. *Picking only makes it worse.*

It turns out there's a difference between complaining and criticism. I read that in a book about relationship building.

Complaints are healthy. And specific. For example, "I feel annoyed that you didn't put gas in the car when you said you would. Could you fill the tank this afternoon?" Criticism is more global and oftentimes involves attacking a partner's character or personality. For example, when I came home with an ink stain on my work slacks and Bruce told me to blot it with Rubbing Alcohol or, if that didn't work, I could create a paste with two parts vinegar and three parts cornstarch, I blurted, "You're such a know-it-all!"

For that, I had to thumb through my relationship building worksheets and deduct five points from my Good Partner column for Criticizing.

Fortunately, when I attacked Bruce's personality with the know-it-all comment that day, he replied, "I am not! You're the only one who's ever called me that!"

Then I was able to deduct three points from Bruce's Good Partner column for Defensiveness. In the margin of his column, I wrote, *minus four additional points for being a know-it-all.*

I'd never thought of myself as a contemptuous person, but according to the relationship book, I needed to take a closer look at that. I said to Bruce, "Oh, like telling me the 'right way' to melt butter in your stainless-steel pan isn't being a know-it-all." I put *right way* in air quotes.

"Sarcasm is an expression of contempt," Bruce told me. He'd been reading the relationship book too.

Minus three points for the air quotes and two points for tone of voice. I was officially in the Crappy Girlfriend column.

I'd never thought of myself as a cruel individual either. Yet, I dangled my independence, my affinity for flight, over Bruce. *I-might-could-leave-at-any-moment...I-might-could-leave-at-*

any-moment… played like a whispered voiceover whenever we argued.

I justified my cruelty with the reminder that living inside Bruce's life tormented me. It seemed that everywhere we went in Stillwater, we ran into Bruce's past. In the Hispanic Food aisle at Walmart one afternoon, Bruce suddenly cowered, pivoting toward a sales rack of canned black beans. In a cloud of floral perfume, a tall, middle-aged woman with pancake makeup and blonde highlights passed by. When she turned toward Cereals, Bruce breathed relief. "We dated a few times right after my divorce," he confessed. "Then she ghosted me."

Later that week, Bruce suggested going out for dinner at a local Chinese restaurant. The Subgum Wonton Soup and Mu Shu Pork were the best ever, he claimed. It was his favorite Chinese restaurant in town, he mentioned. He used to go there often but hadn't been in quite a long time. When we arrived, the hostess greeted him. "Long time, no see!" she said. Then glancing at me and looking back at Bruce, she added, "This time you bring new girl!"

Later, over Edamame and pork dumplings that left a sour taste in my mouth, I said, "I thought we could start a life here together. But we can't even go to Walmart or China Garden without running into your past." Bruce's hazel eyes turned sad. Could he see it in me? My unhappiness?

That night, I thought back to the older couple I'd seen in Ethiopia, a few years back, standing outside the museum in Addis Ababa. The Travelsmiths in their matching cargo pants and sun hats, holding hands and sharing a guidebook on their together adventure. I'd envied them back then. They had each other. They presumably shared a home and meals, shopped and traveled together. As Bruce's bird clock chimed eleven, I wondered, *Were The Travelsmiths really that happy?*

A Good Rain

Years ago, I asked my father, "It's fair to say that you and I are both independent, right?" I said *independent* in an all-caps kind of way. We were sitting on his porch, watching hummingbirds hover over geraniums and horses grazing on lush pasture grass. When he nodded, I followed up. "If we're so self-sufficient, why do we continue searching for a partner?" My father chuckled, held a lit match to his pipe tobacco.

For a while, my father talked about the human propensity for seeking new horizons.

The notion of exploration made sense to me. Flat world, round world. This man. That man.

There were practical aspects of having a partner, we agreed. A person to drive you to your colonoscopy, to sit in the waiting room while you're having oral surgery. A built in plus one at dinner parties and wedding receptions. An automatic emergency contact.

We wondered whether faith was a factor. Faith that something better awaited us. "Like believing in The Hereafter," my father said. "It's the search for Home."

I thought back to the question the Cistercian monk, Brother Doyle, asked during our silent retreat at the Abbey many years ago -- "What comes to mind when you think of Home?" His answer – "Freedom" – still baffled me.

I asked my father, "What's Home to you?"

"Where I am," he said.

Where I was -- Bruce's house in Stillwater, Oklahoma – continued to bear little resemblance, in my mind, to Home.

On the morning of the 2016 Presidential election in which nearly 950,000 Oklahoman voters pulled the Trump lever, I drank my coffee from a Rock the Pantsuit mug. At a voting site in Stillwater, I held open the door for an elderly woman holding a cane. She carried a camouflage handbag on which she'd stuck a bumper sticker – *Hillary for prison 2016*. Beside me in line, a middle-aged man held a squirming toddler. "I want down," the little boy said. "Great Gran Paw-Paw, I want down!" A lanky young man in starched jeans wore a black baseball cap – *Build the Wall.*

Later, in Bruce's living room, I pointed to a mountain of books, fifty or more, piled on the floor. The built-in bookshelves at the other end of the room stood half empty. I offered to shelve the books, but Bruce declined. It was on his to-do list, he explained, but most likely he wouldn't get around to it anytime soon. "I need time to organize the books in a logical manner," Bruce said.

"How long have the books been on the floor?" I asked.

"Two years."

Bruce's living room had become a designated landing strip for household items in need of relocation. Large plastic bins filled with Bruce's old clothes that needed to be sorted and donated. Rolled up rugs. Boxes of old records and cassette tapes. It wasn't that Bruce was lazy. More like paralyzed from over-thinking. *Should my Greek literature share a shelf with Quaker philosophy?*

Despite my shriveled ovaries, I felt a primal urge to nest. Clear out debris. Cozy up the space. Place the blue candles beside the silver lamp on the end table because doing so created aesthetic pleasantry. That brought nerve-wracking past mojo into the mix for Bruce. Years before, his then-wife had hired an interior decorator. The decorator stacked Bruce's books on the shelves according to size, shape, and color for "balance." "I couldn't find squat!" Bruce told me.

Offer: I'll take the clothes to Goodwill for you. I'll shelve those books this Saturday. I'll carry those rugs upstairs so they'll be stored out of the way until you decide where they should go. I'll put the boxes of records in the guest room. *If I'm going to live here, I need some control over my environment. I want to make it feel like home.*

Counter-offer: I'll get to it. It's on my to-do list. I just need to find the right time. *It's my home too, woman. What's next? Fluffy curtains?*

Build the Wall.

Many days, our attempts at negotiating shared living space in Bruce's house left me feeling frustrated and exasperated. Then there were days I'd observe Bruce in action -- Bruce the knowledgeable homeowner. Bruce the caring partner. Bruce the furry man standing in front of me wearing jeans and a tool belt -- and I'd have a breakthrough.

A mouse had babies inside the bathroom wall. It took us a while to figure that one out. "What's that smell?" we'd ask, as we passed the bathroom door. Then we'd remind one another to turn the fan on next time.

Eventually, Bruce called a plumber, assuming a backed-up sewer line. The plumber told Bruce, "It smells like something died in here."

"It wasn't me," Bruce said. "I turned on the fan last time."

"In the wall," the plumber clarified. "Something died in your wall."

And that very afternoon, with hammer and saw, Bruce embarked on his man of the house project. Then the terrible smell was gone.

There were other grotesque tasks that my man in the house took on. Fishing long hairs out of a clogged shower drain, for example. Discarding a decomposed squirrel carcass. Hosing week-old chicken fat from the bottom of the trash container.

"Would you mind?" I'd ask, pointing to the spider scaling the bedroom wall. Or the pile of racoon scat near the corner of the deck. "Would you mind?"

Bruce didn't mind. Cleaning up gross things. Blowing leaves. Inflating tires. Changing oil. Fixing hinges. Mowing grass. Repairing sprinklers. Tightening lug nuts. Replacing furnace filters. Charging batteries.

Then one day I inquired, "I think the red carpet that's rolled up in the living room might look nice in the dining room. Would you mind if I moved it there?"

That, he minded.

"I could use more space for my shoes and clothes," I said. "But the closet shelves are filled with miscellaneous boxes. Would you mind if I put those boxes in the attic?"

He minded.

"It's a good thing I didn't bring more stuff when I moved here," I told Bruce pointing to a closet crammed with his muddied boots, pile of outdated sweaters and, was that a Bunsen burner?

"If you'd brought more stuff," Bruce said, "I would have made more room."

Yet rather than room for stuff, I needed space to breathe. "I feel like I'm drowning in things here."

Then one day Bruce had a conversation with a wiseman. A fellow Quaker who served on the same nonprofit board as Bruce. Bruce vented his troubles to the wiseman. Told the wiseman that His Love had said she liked his house back when they were dating. But now that she lived there, she wanted to change everything. His Love wanted to paint over his green walls. Move the NordicTrack out of the dining room. Donate the wicker baskets stacked in the corner of the foyer. Get rid of the rusted shelving unit in the breezeway. Clear the junk mail, tins of paper clips and old newspapers off the kitchen counter.

Change can be difficult, said the wiseman. It sounds like you have a decision to make. What's more important? Your Love or Your Possessions?

Bruce had a breakthrough of his own.

Superfluous item by superfluous item, Bruce began sorting and de-cluttering. He donated the canvas tent and camping stove he hadn't used since the 1990's and the corduroy pants he hadn't worn in two decades. He transported a rusted mattress frame and boxes of cracked floor tiles to the town dump. He gave away the fake Christmas tree that stood in the corner of his attic and the 8-quart chafing dishes that occupied the top shelf of his pantry. He found homes for the records and cassettes he no longer listened to, and the badminton set he no longer used. He filled his car with bins of old board games and knick knacks, a fishbowl and macramé plant hangers.

My lungs filled with air.

Over dinner one evening, Bruce told me he'd made an appointment to take my car to Firestone for a tune-up and brake check. "I want your car in perfect working order," he said. Then added, "It carries precious cargo."

I-might-could-stay-here... I-might-could-stay-here...

Soon after, over Christmas break, Bruce and I traveled to Costa Rica, our first real vacation together. We walked in the cloud forest wearing yellow rain ponchos and binoculars around our necks. Through the lens of a 60x zoom spotting scope, we spotted a Quetzal. Its red breast puffed, in the shape of a heart, from beneath blue wing feathers.

Toward the end of our trip, Bruce and I drove to Cano Negro, past orange groves and riverside gallery forests then became geographically disoriented along partially flooded, unpaved roads. Eventually and somehow, we happened upon a boat tour. It was just the two of us with a guide – a gentleman highly knowledgeable about the wetlands and wildlife. His English was limited. My Spanish rusty. He pointed out tiny frogs and longnose bats on trees and brown-throated sloth on high up branches. "Wow!" we said. He pointed to a Pygmy Kingfisher, Sandpipers, Sungrebes, a Yellow-Breasted Crake. "Wow!" I squatted at the bow of the small boat for a while, mesmerized by the beauty. Then joined Bruce at the starboard as he alternately raised his binoculars and flipped through pages of his *Birds of Costa Rica* book. "Is that a Nicaraguan Seed-Finch?" "Wow! Wow!"

We'd paid the guide for two hours but drifted along for three. At the end of our voyage, standing on the dock, he waved away our offer to pay for the extra hour. Smiling, he said, "You two love nature."

"We do. We do."

A while back, steeped in frustration, I'd asked Bruce a question.

"What's our shared vision?"

Now, in turn, Bruce asked a question of me. "How about marriage?"

And rather than fear, I experienced a deep sense of settling. Like freshly tilled garden soil after a good, soaking rain.

Brooding Together

One dreary Saturday afternoon, Bruce and I drove to Tractor Supply to buy seed and suet for the bird feeders. We arrived to find a banner strung above the store entrance. *Chick Days!*

In the polestar of Tractor Supply were six silver livestock troughs with heat lamps hovering like robotic eyes. Two brooding tanks housed ducklings – lemon-downed and orange-billed like sugar coated citrus candies. In the other four tanks were tiny three-day-old chickens of varying breeds – black Barred Rocks, yellow Buff Orpingtons, Rhode Island Reds. Laminated signs labeled the breeds and read, "Pullets" or "Straight Run."

Bruce and I peered into the brooding tank with Barred Rocks and Buffs. Roughly fifty fuzzy chicks the colors of onyx and canned corn navigated the crowded tank like honeybees in a hive.

Glancing at the signs on the chick tanks, I asked, "So what's the difference between 'straight run' and 'pullet'?"

I'd asked the question to Bruce, but a beefy-shouldered woman holding a bag of Flock Party Corn and Mealworm piped up. "Straight runs are both hens and roosters," she said, leaning in front of Bruce to look me in the eye. "Pullets are girls."

She explained that you can't tell the difference between hens and roosters until around the age of five months, when a rooster will start to crow. "Folks'll say you can tell the difference by lookin' at their combs or tail feathers…" Her eyes, close set like a falcon's, narrowed. "Bunch of bull crap," she said. The woman went on to say that, since most people wanted hens for egg-laying and didn't want roosters crowing at "four frickin' o'clock in the mornin'," the pullets had been "sexed" to determine that they were, indeed, female.

Tucking a bag of Chick Grit underneath her arm, she said, "I won't do that to my chicks." Then added, "I think it hurts their tiny lady parts." Bruce took a step back while the woman offered details. "What they do is hold 'em upside down and open their hole." I rubbed my forehead. *Oh, boy. Here we go!* She jutted out one hip to balance her sack. "That's right. They spread open their little hole and look right into it. If there's a pimple down there, it's a rooster."

A tall, lanky Tractor Supply employee approached the tanks. Bruce and I advanced toward him with eager eyes, signaling to the chicken woman that we had business to attend to and, therefore, no more time to chew the fat about detection of pudenda on domesticated fowl. The employee ran a hand through his unwashed brown hair and nodded in my direction. "Ma'am," he said, then turned to Bruce, "Sir." The handwritten nametag stuck to the breast pocket of his plaid shirt read, *Kenadee*. "How can I help you two today?" Kenadee asked, offering a yellowed-toothed smile.

"Well," Bruce began. "Can you tell us about the Buff Orpingtons and Barred Rocks?"

"Friendly, cold-hardy birds," said Kenadee. "Good egg-layers, too."

In the flock, I noticed one cream and charcoal-colored chick in the brooder, shouldering its way between the swarm of solid yellow and black chicks at the feeder. "What's the deal with that one?" I asked. "That's not a Buff or a Barred, is it?"

Kenadee squinted his eyes. "Huh. Could be a mutated Buff, I suppose. Or maybe a Leghorn." He bent at the waist to get a closer look. "Yeah, probably a Leghorn. Got put in the wrong tank." He scratched his chin. "Happens."

I slid my arm under Bruce's elbow. "They really are cute."

"Oh, yeah." Bruce nodded. "Chickens are fun. We raised a bunch in our backyard years ago."

"Really? You raised chickens?" That was the kind of discovery that occurred when, like Bruce and me, two people met at midlife. Each of us had past married lives that spanned twenty or thirty years before we ever knew that one another existed on the planet. Just when I thought I knew everything about Bruce, he'd casually mention that he sustained himself on frozen beef pot pies for three months when he lived in New York City or that he once had two dogs, both named Rex. Or, in this case, that he'd raised chickens.

"Yep. Built a little hutch," Bruce said. "Gathered fresh eggs every morning…" Bruce lowered his voice and added, "Technically, our yard is not zoned for chickens, but we had hens – no crowing roosters. Gave our neighbors free eggs. No one cared."

"Sounds nice," I said, perusing the tanks. All at once, I envisioned me and my fowl-knowledgeable man engaging in a together-hobby. A joint poultry project. A shared vision in which we became well-loved by neighbors and colleagues as we freely dispensed the dozens of fresh eggs that would, eventually, pop out of our hens' lady holes.

Ten chirping babies huddled inside the small, cardboard carton that I temporarily placed, along with a sack of Chick Starter and birdseed suet cakes, on the kitchen counter. It was easy to create a home for tiny chicks. I set a box beside the loveseat in the TV room, scattered a layer of pine shavings on the bottom and set up an adjustable heat lamp to provide 90 degrees for their first week of life, then 85 degrees for their second week, and so on. After setting water and food silos in the corners of the box, I cupped my hand around each chick in the carton. Held it up to face me before setting it in its new environment. "Chup, chup," I said. They tilted their tiny heads side to side. Blinked their circle eyes. "Chup, chup," they answered.

There's a show I used to watch called *Tiny House*, in which persons keen on transitioning toward a minimalistic lifestyle, were shown three houses – on average, 100 to 400 square feet in size. Most of these potential buyers had made the mental shift to downsizing and tiny living, and provided a cheerful, on-camera pledge to purchase one of the three homes. Occasionally, however, one of them – usually the six-foot-tall husband – would drag their big feet. They'd step into the manufactured house the size of a common shed, sit slumped on the pulled-down trundle bed and exclaim, "It's so small!" *Well, yeah,* I'd think. *It's a Tiny House.*

Our chicks toddled about, fully content, in their small box for two weeks. Then overnight, it seemed, they morphed into gargoyles the size of gourds, resembling the dinosaurs from which they'd descended. Complete with claws, dander and starchy, ragged feathers poking through soft down.

At that point, flock dynamics turned to drama as they postured battles in their too-tight living quarters, pecking one another away from the food dish, belly bumping their way through territorial disputes. I purchased a four-foot-long wardrobe box from U-Haul, lay it on its side, cut open the top with a razor, and transported the chicks into their upsized living space.

When our gargoyles outgrew that box and started balking like the rangy husband on *Tiny House*, Bruce and I returned to Tractor Supply and purchased a coop. The Deluxe Ranch Chicken Coop (assembly required) featuring a tin roof and elevated wooden nesting hutch inside a spacious, framed courtyard with meshed wire walls. The instruction booklet which accompanied the coop stated that two people, rather than one, were recommended for assembling the product. Bruce and I attached Front and Back Run Panels, screwed the Support Arm onto the nesting box lid, affixed a mesh floor to the coop to keep predators, such as racoons and opossums, out. Then pounded two-by-two posts into the ground, strung yards of fencing, built a simple gate with latch and our chicken estate was complete.

We placed two vinyl chairs in the chicken yard with a small, round table in between. Our Chicken Bistro, we called it.

"It'd be nice to have land," Bruce said one evening as we sat in our Chicken Bistro eating nuts from a bowl and drinking red wine. "Space for a big garden, room for more chickens..."

Then Bruce and I got thinking about selling his house and buying a place with acreage, a homestead on a plot of prairie land. We weren't fully chewing on the idea yet, more like gumming it every now and again. We'd open our laptops, scan realtors' websites featuring properties with land for sale, and find ourselves saying things like, "Ooh, wouldn't it be great to have a pond?"

"Holy crap," Bruce muttered one Sunday afternoon, gazing at the virtual tour of a forty-acre parcel. "It has a windmill!" Then our imaginations airdropped us into a simple life, the kind unplagued by aggravating emails and dour newscasts. An existence in which I read in front of the fireplace while bread baked over an open hearth, and Bruce strolled our expanse of loam, a fishing rod propped against one shoulder.

That same day, I clicked on a listing of a red brick Colonial, its windows accented with shutters the color of buttermilk. On the front porch, ceramic planters filled with flowering Hibiscus stood on either side of a tall double-door painted pineapple-yellow. The yard was spacious and lush with Juniper, Nandina, Rose of Sharon, Monkey grass. It's a nice house, I found myself thinking, but I'd go bolder with the shutter color – a slate blue, perhaps -- and the bright yellow door would have to go.

I looked around the house in which I currently lived. The house where home improvement decisions had been made by Bruce and his ex-wife. Over the course of three decades, they'd had the kitchen remodeled, the upstairs re-carpeted, a porch added on. They'd painted hallways and stairwells and hung old family portraits. Decorated living spaces with furniture passed down from their great uncles and grandparents.

For me, a relative newcomer, to suggest tearing off wallpaper, re-painting rooms, or moving grandmother's bureau out of the dining room and into the attic felt like a delicate matter. Those patterns and colors and family fixtures had taken up residence well before I'd arrived with my vision of different hues, textures and focal points added into the mix. I understood the resistance. An abrupt re-arranging of a person's space could reek of intrusion. Yet how would I find my way to calling this house my "home" without the latitude to vocalize personal opinion or creative expression?

It seemed that making room for two lives coming together, inside a house owned by one, was more complicated than emptying a dresser drawer and clearing closet shelves. I now realized it had more to do with providing space for both partners' voices to reverberate from wall to wall, floor to ceiling, at equal volume.

I knew then it was time to take our house hunting from theoretical to concrete. In order to create a home, a life, here in Oklahoma with Bruce, we'd need to start with a clean canvas.

No Brainer

"Hands down," Bruce's colleague told him. "Brenda with Prairie Star Realty is the best."

When we first started house hunting, Bruce and I considered properties in need of TLC. "A fixer-upper with character would be fine," I clarified. And Bruce said that's how people could describe him.

"So much potential!" Brenda would say as we walked through vacant houses, trying to look past dark, paneled bedrooms, dated kitchen linoleum and olive-green countertops. "You'll want to completely gut the kitchen, of course," Brenda would tell us. "Install new cupboards, a large granite-top island. You could tear out the shag carpet in the living room and put in hardwood floors, replace the sliding glass doors with French..."

"But how much would that cost?" Bruce and I would repeat. "Ballpark. How much?"

Then Brenda showed us better maintained properties with acreage and ponds. Houses in which the kitchens were not in need of gutting. Where walls didn't need to be knocked down. "You'll want to add your own touches," Brenda would say as we stood in the living room of an updated farmhouse. "But it's move-in ready." Bruce and I would meander around those country lots feeling disoriented, sniffing the air.

"How far is the nearest gas station?" we'd ask. "Where do people grocery shop around here?"

After reining in our search, I decided that the trick with house hunting was to stay focused on the big picture. Location, square footage, room layout, number of bathrooms, kitchen functionality, lot size. When viewing a home, avoid getting distracted by details of the current inhabitants' lives.

In a three-bedroom ranch, we entered a cathedral-ceilinged family room. "I used to have a sofa just like that," Bruce said. "Oh, look! Beanbag chairs!"

In a cedar shingled split-level, Bruce opened a closet door in the spare bedroom. Hanging from the rack were several martial arts uniforms. "The owner must be a black belt," Bruce said. "Is that Judo or Taekwondo?"

"Remember what we talked about, Bruce?" I said in the tone of an elementary teacher talking to a second grader. "It's helpful to stay focused on the big picture."

At times, Brenda relayed the sellers' histories. One couple was relocating to Wisconsin for a better job opportunity. Another young family wanted to be closer to their kid's grandparents. A retired couple was downsizing and had put an offer in on a condominium.

We entered a Cape Cod with second story window dormers peaked like dazed eyes. An elderly woman had put it on the market a few weeks earlier. She planned to move north, Brenda told us, to be nearer her daughter. In the master bathroom, linen closet shelves were filled with Styrofoam heads in wigs. "Cancer," I said. "Gosh, I hope she ends up being okay."

Bruce put his arm around my shoulder, and I patted his hand. Then he raised an eyebrow. "Whatever happened to focusing on the big picture, Cakes?"

We soon realized that something bigger than the big picture was at play each time we walked through the front door of a house for sale. "It's a great location," I'd say. "The square footage is ideal, and the layout is well thought out…"

Brenda would beam. "And the kitchen's breakfast nook is adorable."

"But…" I'd bite my lip and Bruce would nod. "It's just not…"

"Speaking to us," Bruce would say.

Later, I said to Bruce, "It's funny. Houses have mojo. All the boxes can be checked off, but if that magical charm is missing, it's just not going to work."

We both agreed that house hunting was a lot like dating.

"You'll know it's the right house," Brenda told us. "When you walk in and can imagine yourselves there."

Eventually, we looked at a two-story, flat-faced Colonial with a rugged gray rock exterior reminding me of the face of a mountain. It had a wood fireplace in the living room and large windows in the kitchen. "If we hung bird feeders over there," Bruce said, pointing to a shady area near the back yard deck, "we could watch from the kitchen table."

There was a spare bedroom upstairs, its walls a bright lime green. "You know, with a few coats of paint," I said, "this could be a nice home office."

We could see ourselves there.

We walked through the backyard, two acres with shrubs, mature trees, and an old fence around its perimeter. "Wow! What a great yard for chickens!" Bruce said. Then we both felt a little sad.

Our house search had begun with the focus of chicken-keeping in mind. We'd say to Brenda, "The house is great, but the yard is too small for chickens." Or "We love this neighborhood, but is it zoned for chickens?"

Now that we found the house that spoke to us with an excellent yard in which to raise our original flock of ten chickens, we were down to one hen.

Our sole survivor was Iggy. A Barred Rock with a pointy, red comb that sat atop her gray head feathers like a party hat.

Over the past few months, in spite of Bruce and me steadfastly securing our chickens in their wooden hutch soon after sunset each evening, we'd lost most of our chickens to predators that struck during daylight hours. We can't blame them, Bruce and I agreed. Those racoons and foxes and hawks who'd eaten our birds. We loved chicken too. Yet, each time we wept.

Together, Bruce and I embarked on the overwhelming task of putting his house on the market and preparing to move. In spite of Bruce's earlier efforts to sort and de-clutter, there remained mountains of stuff.

Question: How many trips to Goodwill does it take to put a dent in a houseful of stuff acquired over the course of thirty-two years? Cupboards full of old thermoses, travel mugs and wicker serving trays. Boxes of baseball caps, stained work shirts and wool socks bore through by moths. Moldy camping mats, dusty blankets, plastic Christmas holly stored in the attic. The toaster oven and Bunsen burner discovered on a way-up-high closet shelf.

Answer: No end in sight.

I irritated Bruce with the same questions over and over. When was the last time you wore this tweed suit? How long have these sweaters sat in boxes? When was the last time you actually used this? I'd downsized to the point of fitting all my personal belongings into a compact car. Tiny car living. I had little mercy.

Me: Have you used that tennis racket since 1975?

Bruce: It can be re-strung.

Me: When was the last time you broke a sweat on that NordicTrack?

Bruce: It's been a while, but I'm breaking a sweat now.

It was around that time that Bruce began making mention of my military past. When Bruce and I had first dated, spending long, lazy weekends revealing our personal histories, he was intrigued by my service in the Army Reserves. When he learned that I'd ended up serving for eight years, the last half of those years working as a drill sergeant, he was downright fascinated. "Tell me more," he'd say, and I'd talk about the 0400h wake-up calls. The smell of greasy eggs and grits in the mess hall. Night marches with ruck sacks on our backs and camouflaged helmets -- *steel pots* they call them -- on our heads. I'd talk about disassembling and re-assembling our M-16 rifles. Pulling pins at the grenade range. Teaching trainees drill and ceremony and hand-to-hand combat skills. Bruce, being Quaker, was a pacifist, but he loved my military lingo. *Dropping trainees for push-ups. Dogging them with grass drills.*

Me: I could use a hand moving the mirror out of the attic.

Bruce: Yes, Drill Sergeant.

Me: Do you think we can pack up the garage this weekend?

Bruce: Yes, Drill Sergeant.

Me: I'd like to finish taping up those boxes before lunch.

Bruce: Yes, Drill Sergeant.

Me: Your drill sergeant joke is getting old. Is that a peanut butter sandwich you're eating?

Bruce: Gulp.

A few weeks before our move, Bruce and I were pushing our empty grocery cart into the return corral at Food Pyramid when the mathematician and his set designer wife pulled their jeep into a parking space nearby. Bruce filled them in on our house hunting adventures. Told them about the home we looked at in which the family room had been turned into a saloon. "A real saloon!" Bruce said. Full wet bar. Shelves filled with vodkas, whiskeys, bourbons, rums. A mock cash register. Bar stools and wild west murals.

"Holy smokes," said the mathematician, chuckling. He smiled at the two of us. "So I hear congratulations are in order."

"Yes, congratulations!" said the set designer then wriggled her fingers at my cell phone. "Wedding photos?"

Bruce and I had chosen to wed with an eye toward simplicity. Not exactly a grab-some-grocery-store-flowers-and-go-to-the-courthouse kind of deal, but a quiet ceremony. We exchanged vows at Bruce's house, in front of a minister and three witnesses, on our patio decorated with potted Hibiscus and Mums. Champagne and cake in the kitchen afterwards. "No white gown?" the set designer asked, studying a photo of me in a silver, tea-length dress.

"Not my first rodeo," I told her. Was I sounding Oklahoman?

"Have you put an offer in on a house yet?" the mathematician asked.

"We'll close on a place in less than a month," Bruce said. "Our commute to work will be a lot longer, but we'll only need to drive to the university a few days a week…" Our new house was located in an Oklahoma City suburb, about forty miles south of Stillwater.

"Big change," the mathematician said.

"Yes, it will be. But after we got married," Bruce said, "we realized it was time to sell." I detected a tinge of apology in Bruce's voice. Concerned that he'd disappointed his old friends by selling off a parcel of their shared history.

"So, let me get this straight," the set designer began. "You sold the house you'd lived in for over thirty years so that you and Laurie could find a new house together?"

Bruce nodded. "Yep, I guess that sums it up."

Smiling, the set designer said, "No brainer."

Home to Roost

The last box we packed in Bruce's old house was the first box we unpacked in our new together house. It was lined with pine shavings, punched with air holes, and contained our bossy Barred Rock, Iggy, who squawked her indignation for the entirety of the forty-mile car ride.

We settled Iggy into her new environment -- her private deluxe coop with wooden hutch situated on two acres. Iggy scratched at dirt and leaves in search of bugs, roosted beneath thick hollies and checked in with us often, pecking at the windowpane when she saw Bruce or me in the kitchen. She missed her flock.

Mornings, we handfed her sunflower seeds. Evenings, we held her on our laps, scratched under her chin. We spread an extra layer of straw in her hutch and set a ceramic egg in her nesting box, hoping she'd feel less alone.

"It takes four seasons," a friend once told me. "To feel at home in a new place."

But in spite of being relatively new to Oklahoma, it had taken me four days. From the moment we moved in, I'd hit our together house running. Unpacking boxes. Hanging up clothes.

Unrolling rugs. Arranging furniture. Shelving books. Creating a home.

On weekend mornings, Bruce and I would sit at the kitchen table -- watching cardinals and finches perch at the feeders and Iggy pace at the window and yammer for attention -- talking through possibilities.

"Will we plant Turk's Caps in the side yard this spring?" I'd wonder aloud.

"Sounds good to me," Bruce would say. "But Begonias might do better in the shade."

"We could put down cedar mulch," I'd add. "But a stone mulch might look great there."

Bruce would sip coffee and nod. "Might could."

Sliding paint swatches in front Bruce, I'd ask, "What do you think? Should I paint the living room White Truffle or Saybrook Sage?"

"You have a better eye for those things," Bruce would tell me.

"Or we could go a bit brighter with Palladian Blue. Or more thoughtful with Mindful Gray…"

"Your call, Cakes," Bruce would say, smiling. "After all, it's your house."

The storm came up fast that night. A system barreling south from Stillwater, colliding with a second system heading north from Norman. Our new home was located in between. Lightning flashed. Rain poured. Hail pounded. Then the siren went off. "Put your shoes on!" Bruce yelled. "Tornado!"

Dizzy with fear, I grabbed our storm bag with flashlight and blanket and ran outside in torrential downpour to our underground shelter. I pulled at the cellar door handle, but the hinge was stiff. The door didn't open. I dropped the storm bag and pulled hard with both hands. It budged but remained stuck. My arms and legs shaking, I gulped down breaths.

Suddenly, Bruce was behind me. He grabbed the handles. Pulled open the door. Clutching the bag, I scrambled down the steep cement steps as Bruce pulled the shelter door closed and locked it in place. I sat in the shelter catching shallow breaths, rainwater dripping down my neck. In the wake of my fear, I felt tremendous relief to be sitting safely underground. And, especially, to be there with Bruce -- my husband, my love, my tornado expert in residence.

We sat silently for a moment, our hands on one another's knees then we faced each other and said in unison, "I hope Iggy's okay."

Reaching into the storm bag, I grabbed a flashlight, flicked it on and looked down at Bruce's sneakers.

"What's the deal about putting shoes on?" I asked Bruce. "If there's a tornado coming, shouldn't we get in the shelter as fast as possible?"

Bruce put his arm around my shoulders. "If a tornado hit our house, there'd be a lot of debris with nails and glass to walk through." The tornado siren stopped, and Bruce held up his palms. "All clear."

I held up my bare feet and wiggled my toes. "Since we made it out of here alive," I teased, "I'll put spare sneakers in the shelter, so next time we won't have to worry about it."

"Makes sense," Bruce said. "If it weren't for the brown recluse that would love to make a home in those sneakers down here."

"Brown recluse?" I asked.

"A spider that lives here. Its bite is poisonous."

God, I had so much to learn about living in Oklahoma.

*

Oklahoma winter nights could drop into the single digits. At two o'clock in the morning, I sat in the living room, a fleece blanket wrapped around my shoulders, staring into the glow of an incubator containing nine eggs. Watching. Waiting. One of the eggs had pipped after dinner. The chick's yellow egg tooth pecked at shell then rested. Knocked for a while more, chiseling an opening the shape of a puzzle piece. Then with one heave, the shell cracked open. The wet chick rolled on its side and breathed open air.

Bruce was there too. "Oh," we whispered together. Bruce was watching as he lay on the sofa, his right leg propped on a pillow with bags of frozen peas and corn set on top of his knee and shin.

Four weeks earlier, Bruce had undergone knee replacement surgery. An orthopedist had removed his kneecap and cartilage and replaced it with a joint made of Titanium. "Titanium!" I'd said to Bruce after one of the doctor's appointments leading up to the surgery. "My superhero."

But after the surgery, Bruce didn't feel like a superhero. He tiny-stepped around the house wearing compression hose and gel-treaded socks navigating his walker around the sofa and ingesting medications, trying to stay on top of the pain.

Bruce's old, arthritic knee had spoken in breaths of dull pain. The chronicity of the discomfort was tiresome, but its familiarity had made it bearable for far too long. He'd limped along for years, receiving corticosteroid shots and platelet-rich plasma injections. His new Titanium knee wailed in bouts of deep ache, which quieted every so often when numbed with opioids and ice. Then its wailing resumed.

Every room of our house became occupied with post-surgical paraphernalia. A Dual-Release folding walker. Ortho-Ease grip cane. Shower seat. CPM Motion Machine. Incentive Spirometer. Urinals. Our home décor had gone from something vaguely resembling Boho Modern Country to Reimagined Design, Convalescent Inspired.

Our topics of conversation, rather than touching on work, politics, and birdwatching, now centered on basic creature comforts.

I asked Bruce many questions. "Would you like a glass of water?" "Do you need more ice?" "I'm going to the store. Anything besides soup that might taste good to you?"

"Yes, please." "Yes, please." "More chicken soup."

"How did you sleep last night?" I asked Bruce each morning.

"Up half the night."

"What time will the physical therapist be here?"

"Around noon," I think.

Since Bruce was on pain medication that had an unfortunate side effect, there was one question I asked repeatedly for ten days straight. "Did you poop yet?" "Have you pooped?"

"God, I wish."

Setbacks are a part of it, the physician's assistant had warned. Bruce would have a good day or two. Navigate the kitchen without using his walker. Bend his leg at a 45-degree angle without pain. Wake up semi-refreshed and make scrambled eggs and toast. He'd take a shower. I'd clip his toenails. We'd talk about something besides pain med dosage and bowel movements. "Progress," we'd say. Then unrelenting pain again and sleepless nights.

As dismal as that felt at times, we found comfort in our teamwork. Bruce and I were in this together. Just as we were the evening the tornado siren went off. And the night we watched in awe as the eggs in our incubator hatched, then gently cupped each new life in the palms of our hands.

With time and physical therapy and icing his new joint, Bruce experienced a cautiously optimistic break in his suffering. About three weeks after his surgery, Bruce showered then changed into something other than flannel pajamas and robe. I was sitting at the kitchen table working on lesson plans when Bruce entered the room, maneuvering his walker, wearing navy-blue sweatpants and matching sweatshirt. He'd clearly owned those clothes for a while. The fabric of the heavyweight cotton pants was pilled and, down the sides of the pantlegs and the sleeves of the zippered sweatshirt, were wide, red racing stripes. First, I felt proud. "You're in your action clothes!" I said. Then I wondered how, months earlier, that hideous 1990's sweat pant ensemble had made it past me and into a moving box.

About a month later, Bruce and I received an invitation to a Homeowner's Association (HOA) meeting. I quickly chalked up the meeting to a likely waste of time. Our Association fees were a mere $75.00 per year. I didn't feel the need to weigh in on fiscal decisions regarding neighborhood improvement. Let them spend our seventy-five bucks however they wanted. Bruce, however, was all excited about the prospect of meeting people. Besides, he told me, it would give him an excuse to shower and put on real pants.

Our house was built in a neighborhood developed in the 1970's, with lot sizes ranging from two to five acres. "It's a mixed neighborhood," our realtor had told us, meaning a mix of country folk and suburban types. Several yards had fenced areas once used to paddock a horse or two. Back when the neighborhood was established, the outlying area consisted mostly of farms, grassy fields, a post office and school district, a few churches. Now, within a three-mile drive were restaurants and nail salons, an Uptown Grocers and Hobby Lobby. While a few families in the community owned a horse or a pony, most yards had children's swing sets, dog houses, and vegetable gardens. I'd never imagined myself living in housing development to begin with, let alone one in which most houses had pickup trucks backed into their driveways. But, then again, I'd never imagined myself living in Oklahoma with a man – the man – I somehow found and who somehow found me.

The HOA meeting was held in the pastor's office of a nearby church. When I entered the room packed with gray-haired people in nylon slacks seated on folding chairs, my first thought was, *Everyone here is so old!* Then Bruce came clunking in with his walker.

The volunteer running the meeting started with a shout-out to Ethel for planting the beautiful Azaleas near the neighborhood sign. Then some complaining ensued. What could we do about the neighbors who left unsightly trash receptacles at the curb for three or four days after pickup? And could someone talk to the neighbor who keeps letting his Pitbull-mix roam off-leash? And what about that messy tangle of trees near the road at the corner? Could someone offer to bring their chain saw over and cut them down?

"What about the birds?" Bruce and I thought out loud and people looked at us quizzically. "If you cut down the trees, what about the birds?"

*

Our own birds were faring well. More than four seasons had passed, and our hatched chicks along with day-old chicks we'd bought from Tractor Supply, were now mature birds. Our fenced-in back yard with abundant shrubs and evergreens that our chickens roosted under was proving to be a far safer environment than Bruce's former yard in Stillwater. Our hens, so far, were thriving.

The flock of thirteen included Black Australorps, white Brahma's, and Golden Laced Wyandottes. Iggy was smallest in stature, yet highest in the pecking order. She strutted across the yard in her red party hat, squawking orders at her newfound brood.

The surprising thing about chickens was that they ate almost anything. Guacamole, yogurt, watermelon, bologna. Our hens, who were laying eggs daily, seemed delighted to devour our leftovers.

On a warm, early autumn afternoon, Bruce and I carried plastic bowls of chicken treats to our back yard. "Chickens!" Bruce called toward the way back. "Chickens!" And from the thickly shrubbed perimeter, our brood came trundling toward us.

We set down the bowls heaped with leftover steamed rice, pieces of deli ham and globs of chunky peanut butter and the flock clamored and clucked and attacked the food like a school of Grouper on Cheez Whiz.

"Barbarians," I teased. "Relax. There's plenty for everyone." They reminded me of the way my siblings and I used to eat when we came home from school "starved" and my mother dropped a Duncan Hines cake on the kitchen counter. Did we even use forks? My mother would mumble something about manners. *Gosh, I hope you don't eat like that at other people's houses.* But she knew we reserved our boorish behavior for home.

"Let's have a seat, Cakes," Bruce suggested. We headed for the deck and eased into two of the four chairs that were part of the steel mesh patio set that Bruce and his ex-wife had purchased decades earlier. A year ago, when Bruce and I were deliberating over which household items would make the move and which wouldn't, I'd studied that patio set and said, "It could stand a fresh coat of spray paint." Then added, "But it's functional. Comfortable. And it doesn't have *terrible* mojo."

Most of Bruce's belongings had made the move, of course. His kitchen table, chairs, and grandmother's bureau. His dresser and bed, bookcases, and desk. His wall hangings, area rugs, coffee table and ottoman. Those hokey dishes of his.

In place of Bruce's brown leather bachelor sofa, however, we bought an upholstered sofa and loveseat with soft cushions the color of a skipping stone. At times, on cool mornings, I sat on the loveseat drinking coffee from Bruce's mug, the one hand painted with a cowboy playing the guitar. When my coffee was finished, I'd peer at the bottom of the mug. *Adios,* it read.

Adios. Over the past six years, I'd said so many goodbyes. To my friends and family in upstate New York when I first relocated overseas. To the new friends and colleagues I'd met along the way while traveling in Asia, Africa, Europe, and the Americas.

I'd said goodbye to students at the end of the semester, to chickens who'd crossed the path of a racoon or fox. I'd said adios to Rafael at English Now! in Mexico and to Tom and his *This Is My Life* restaurant display in Fayetteville, Arkansas.

I'd said so long to Stillwater. Farewell to dating. Bid adieu to searching for that special something that felt missing.

As much as I'd reveled in traveling the world with abandon and as grateful as I was for heeding my instinct to seek and explore, I was beginning to welcome the notion that freedom might also have to do with first finding stillness.

"So, what will the rest of our Saturday look like?" Bruce asked, as we watched the chickens peck at the last bits of rice in their bowls.

"It's a beautiful afternoon," I said. "Later, I'll go to Mitch Park. Get in a five-mile jog."

Bruce and I talked about chores we'd wanted to get done. I'd sweep out the chicken coop, wash and refill the water silos. Bruce would prune the ornamental grasses, fix the hinge on the storm shelter door. We chatted about teaching schedules, a new mini-series on Netflix, our preference for shredded bark mulch over wood chips. Our banter about nothing important filled us like a glass of cool, clear water on a warm, sunny day.

"How about dinner out this evening?" Bruce asked. "Pepperoni Grill? Or that new Mediterranean place?" I reached over and placed my hand on Bruce's knee. His surgical scar had faded to a thin, reddish line above the kneecap. Only a mere trace of past trauma was still visible to the eye, the memory of pain softened by time and healing. "Or I could make my revised Beef Stroganoff," Bruce offered. "Without the egg noodles, of course."

Sounds like a good day ahead, we both agreed, and tilted our faces toward sunlight. I'd traveled to many places but had never seen such wide-open sky.

THE END

ACKNOWLEDGMENTS

This book began as a collection of personal essays while attending my MFA program at Queens University of Charlotte. Much gratitude to the faculty and students at Queens for their insightful feedback on earlier versions of this work. Many thanks to the journals in which these essays first appeared, some in partial and edited form: "Keeping Chiripa Alive" in *The Antioch Review*, "Goat Nature" in *The Chattahoochee Review*, "Klepto" in *Catamaran*, and "A Universal Connection" in *Little Patuxent Review*.

Thank you to my mother for her love, sense of humor and bravery. Thank you to my father for his encouragement and inspiration. To my daughter, Gloria, and son-in-law, Connor: much gratitude for spurring me on and for your unrelenting patience and kindness during our evening readings (the wine helped). To my husband, Bruce, for whom I'm eternally grateful: your love, endless support, and faith in my work has meant the world to me.

About the Author

Laurie Woodford is an author, educator, and dog lover. Originally from upstate New York, she now lives in the outskirts of Austin, Texas with her amazing husband, Bruce, and wonder dog, Journey. For more, visit her at www.lauriewoodford.com.

About Unsolicited Press

Unsolicited Press is based out of Portland, Oregon and focuses on the works of the unsung and underrepresented. As a womxn-owned, all-volunteer small publisher that doesn't worry about profits as much as championing exceptional literature, we have the privilege of partnering with authors skirting the fringes of the lit world. We've worked with emerging and award-winning authors such as Shann Ray, Amy Shimshon-Santo, Brook Bhagat, Kris Amos, and John W. Bateman.

Learn more at unsolicitedpress.com. Find us on twitter and instagram.

Printed in the USA
CPSIA information can be obtained
at www.ICGtesting.com
LVHW042305120124
768887LV00058B/1323